PARACLETE MO   LASSICS

Meditations & Devotions

ST. JOHN HENRY NEWMAN

PARACLETE PRESS
BREWSTER, MASSACHUSETTS

2019 First Printing

Meditations and Devotions

Copyright © 2019 by Paraclete Press, Inc.

ISBN 978-1-64060-383-7

Translations of Holy Scripture commonly use the Douay-Rheims, the English translation in common use in the Roman Catholic Church at the time these prayers, devotions, and meditations were originally written. Occasionally, the author has varied these translations slightly.

The Paraclete Press name and logo (dove on cross) are trademarks of Paraclete Press, Inc.

Library of Congress Cataloging-in-Publication Data

Names: Newman, John Henry, 1801-1890, author.
Title: Meditations and devotions / St. John Henry Newman.
Other titles: Meditations and devotions of the late Cardinal Newman (2019)
Description: Brewster, Massachusetts : Paraclete Press, [2019]
Identifiers: LCCN 2019015409 | ISBN 9781640603837 (trade paper)
Subjects: LCSH: Meditations. | Catholic Church--Prayers and devotions.
Classification: LCC BX2182.3 .N45 2019 | DDC 242--dc23
LC record available at https://lccn.loc.gov/2019015409

10 9 8 7 6 5 4 3 2 1

Published by Paraclete Press
Brewster, Massachusetts
www.paracletepress.com

Printed in the United States of America

CONTENTS

EDITORS' INTRODUCTION

Meditations and Devotions was originally published in the first half of the year 1893, just three years after the death of then-Cardinal John Henry Newman. The great nineteenth-century priest, writer, convert, and churchman had long wanted to compose a book of devotions that might be used on a calendar basis, but that project never materialized during his lifetime.

After Newman's death, his literary executor, Fr. William Neville, compiled these meditations and devotions, all of which were part of Newman's own daily spiritual practice. Neville wrote in his original preface:

> It was the Cardinal's custom to note down, in the roughest way, any thought that particularly struck him while meditating, that he might reflect upon it during the day or pursue it in the future; and thus he was led on to enlarge such thoughts, and write out the notes and rewrite them carefully (for he always, he said, could meditate best with a pen in his hand). It is chiefly to this custom of the Cardinal's of keeping the current of holy thoughts within his easy reach, that we owe, it is believed, the preservation of the greater part of this volume.

The book was an immediate success. One contemporary reviewer, in *The Month*, remarked how "the intense sympathy and gentleness which rings through every page, appeals to the sorrowful or wounded heart; and the personal holiness and attitude of loving reverence and gratitude and hope and trust, impart to these meditations the reality and a force of one who pours out his soul before God. For these meditations are essentially a pouring forth of the soul."[1] The profound sense of gentleness, gratitude, and soul in this collection of short writings of prayer and devotion are still clearly felt today.

1 Anonymous reviewer, *The Month*, published by the English Province of the Society of Jesus, Volume 78, August 1893; 417.

vi | *Meditations & Devotions*

There is renewed interest today in now-Saint John Henry Newman. It is our wish that the reissuing of this book will help twenty-first century Christians to rediscover him.

Finally, *Meditations and Devotions* is practical. It is a book that is meant to be used. And it demonstrates the habits and spiritual practices of this remarkable saint of the Church—habits that are perhaps best summarized in this one representative short paragraph:

> If you ask me what you are to do in order to be perfect, I say, first—Do not lie in bed beyond the due time of rising; give your first thoughts to God; make a good visit to the Blessed Sacrament; say the Angelus devoutly; eat and drink to God's glory; say the Rosary well; be recollected; keep out bad thoughts; make your evening meditation well; examine yourself daily; go to bed in good time, and you are already perfect. (see p. 79, below)

ABOUT THE AUTHOR

John Henry Newman (1801–1890) was a poet and theologian, first an Anglican priest, then founder of the Oxford Movement, and later a Catholic priest and cardinal in the Roman Church. The autobiography of this important and controversial figure in the religious history of England in the nineteenth century, *Apologia Pro Vita Sua*, is widely considered to be one of the great Christian classics of the modern era.

Newman was beatified by Pope Benedict XVI in 2010. This book goes to press with Pope Francis planning to canonize St. John Henry Newman in the fall of 2019.

—The Editors

PART ONE

Meditations for the Month of May

MAY 1

MAY, THE MONTH OF PROMISE

Why is May chosen as the month in which we exercise a special devotion to the Blessed Virgin? The first reason is because it is the time when the earth bursts forth into its fresh foliage and its green grass after the stern frost and snow of winter, and the raw atmosphere and the wild wind and rain of the early spring. It is because the blossoms are upon the trees and the flowers are in the gardens. It is because the days have got long, and the sun rises early and sets late. For such gladness and joyousness of external Nature is a fit attendant on our devotion to her who is the Mystical Rose and the House of Gold.

A man may say, "True; but in this climate we have sometimes a bleak, inclement May." This cannot be denied; but still, so much is true that at least it is the month of promise and of hope. Even though the weather happens to be bad, it is the month that begins and heralds in the summer. We know, for all that may be unpleasant in it, that fine weather is coming sooner or later. "Brightness and beautifulness shall," in the Prophet's words, "appear at the end, and shall not lie: if it make delay, wait for it, for it shall surely come, and shall not be slack."

May then is the month, if not of fulfilment, at least of promise; and is not this the very aspect in which we most suitably regard the Blessed Virgin, Holy Mary, to whom this month is dedicated?

The Prophet says, "There shall come forth a rod out of the root of Jesse, and a flower shall rise out of his root" (Isaiah 11:1). Who is the flower but our Blessed Lord? Who is the rod, or beautiful stalk or stem or plant out of which the flower grows, but Mary, Mother of our Lord, Mary, Mother of God?

It was prophesied that God should come upon earth. When the time was now full, how was it announced? It was announced by the

Angel coming to Mary. "Hail, full of grace," said Gabriel, "the Lord is with thee; blessed art thou among women." She then was the sure promise of the coming Savior, and therefore May is by a special title her month.

Introductory

MAY 2
MAY, THE MONTH OF JOY

Why is May called the month of Mary, and especially dedicated to her? Among other reasons there is this, that of the Church's year, the ecclesiastical year, it is at once the most sacred and the most festive and joyous portion. Who would wish February, March, or April to be the month of Mary, considering that it is the time of Lent and penance? Who again would choose December, the Advent season, a time of hope, indeed, because Christmas is coming, but a time of fasting too? Christmas itself does not last for a month; and January has indeed the joyful Epiphany, with its Sundays in succession; but these in most years are cut short by the urgent coming of Septuagesima.

May on the contrary belongs to the Easter season, which lasts fifty days, and in that season the whole of May commonly falls, and the first half always. The great Feast of the Ascension of our Lord into heaven is always in May, except once or twice in forty years. Pentecost, called also Whit-Sunday, the Feast of the Holy Ghost, is commonly in May, and the Feasts of the Holy Trinity and Corpus Christi are in May not unfrequently. May, therefore, is the time in which there are such frequent Alleluias, because Christ has risen from the grave, Christ has ascended on high, and God the Holy Ghost has come down to take His place.

Here then we have a reason why May is dedicated to the Blessed Mary. She is the first of creatures, the most acceptable child of God, the dearest and nearest to Him. It is fitting then that this month should be hers, in which we especially glory and rejoice in His great Providence to us, in our redemption and sanctification in God the Father, God the Son, and God the Holy Ghost.

But Mary is not only the acceptable handmaid of the Lord. She is also Mother of His Son, and the Queen of all Saints, and in this month the Church has placed the feasts of some of the greatest of them, as if to bear her company. First, however, there is the Feast of the Holy Cross, on the 3rd of May; when we venerate that Precious Blood in which the Cross was bedewed at the time of our Lord's Passion. The Archangel St. Michael, and three Apostles, have feast-days in this month: St. John, the beloved disciple, St. Philip and St. James. Seven Popes, two of them especially famous, St. Gregory VII. and St. Pius V.; also two of the greatest Doctors, St. Athanasius and St. Gregory Nazianzen; two holy Virgins especially favored by God, St. Catherine of Siena (as her feast is kept in England), and St. Mary Magdalen of Pazzi; and one holy woman most memorable in the annals of the Church, St. Monica, the Mother of St. Augustine. And above all, and nearest to us in this church, our own Holy Patron and Father, St. Philip, occupies, with his Novena and Octave, fifteen out of the whole thirty-one days of the month.[2] These are some of the choicest fruits of God's manifold grace, and they form the court of their glorious Queen.

---

2 In 1847 St. John Henry Newman was ordained a Catholic priest in Rome and
   joined the Congregation of the Oratory, founded three centuries earlier by
   Saint Philip Neri.

I On the Immaculate Conception

MAY 3

MARY IS THE *VIRGO PURISSIMA*, THE MOST PURE VIRGIN

By the Immaculate Conception of the Blessed Virgin is meant the great revealed truth that she was conceived in the womb of her mother, St. Anne, without original sin.

Since the fall of Adam all mankind, his descendants, are conceived and born in sin. "Behold," says the inspired writer in the Psalm *Miserere*—"Behold, I was conceived in iniquity, and in sin did my mother conceive me" (Psalm 51:5). That sin which belongs to every one of us, and is ours from the first moment of our existence, is the sin of unbelief and disobedience, by which Adam lost Paradise. We, as the children of Adam, are heirs to the consequences of his sin, and have forfeited in him that spiritual robe of grace and holiness which he had given him by his Creator at the time that he was made. In this state of forfeiture and disinheritance we are all of us conceived and born; and the ordinary way by which we are taken out of it is the Sacrament of Baptism.

But Mary *never* was in this state; she was by the eternal decree of God exempted from it. From eternity, God, the Father, Son, and Holy Ghost, decreed to create the race of man, and, foreseeing the fall of Adam, decreed to redeem the whole race by the Son's taking flesh and suffering on the Cross. In that same incomprehensible, eternal instant, in which the Son of God was born of the Father, was also the decree passed of man's redemption through Him. He who was born from Eternity was born by an eternal decree to save us in Time, and to redeem the whole race; and Mary's redemption was determined in that special manner which we call the Immaculate Conception. It was decreed, not that she should be *cleansed* from sin, but that she should, from the first moment of her being, be *preserved* from sin; so that the Evil One never had any part in her. Therefore, she was a child of Adam and Eve as if they had never fallen; she did not share with them their sin; she inherited the gifts and graces (and more than those) which Adam and Eve possessed in Paradise. This is her prerogative, and the foundation of all those salutary truths which are revealed to us concerning her. Let us say then with all holy souls, *Virgin most pure, conceived without original sin, Mary, pray for us.*

I On the Immaculate Conception

MAY 4
MARY IS THE *VIRGO PRÆDICANDA*, THE VIRGIN WHO IS TO BE PROCLAIMED

MARY is the *Virgo Prædicanda*, that is, the Virgin who is to be proclaimed, to be heralded, literally, to be *preached*.

We are accustomed to preach abroad that which is wonderful, strange, rare, novel, important. Thus, when our Lord was coming, St. John the Baptist preached Him; then, the Apostles went into the wide world, and preached Christ. What is the highest, the rarest, the choicest prerogative of Mary? It is that she was without sin. When a woman in the crowd cried out to our Lord, "Blessed is the womb that bare Thee!" (Luke 11:27), He answered, "More blessed are they who hear the word of God and keep it." Those words were fulfilled in Mary. She was filled with grace in order to be the Mother of God. But it was a higher gift than her maternity to be thus sanctified and thus pure. Our Lord indeed would not have become her son *unless* He had first sanctified her; but still, the greater blessedness was to have that perfect sanctification. This then is why she is the *Virgo Prædicanda*; she is deserving to be preached abroad because she never committed any sin, even the least; because sin had no part in her; because, through the fullness of God's grace, she never thought a thought, or spoke a word, or did an action, which was displeasing, which was not most pleasing, to Almighty God; because in her was displayed the greatest triumph over the enemy of souls. Wherefore, when all seemed lost, in order to show what He could do for us all by dying for us; in order to show what human nature, His work, was capable of becoming; to show how utterly He could bring to naught the utmost efforts, the most concentrated malice of the foe, and reverse all the consequences of the Fall, our Lord began, even before His coming, to do His most wonderful act of redemption, in the person of her who was to be His Mother. By the merit of that Blood which was to be shed, He interposed to hinder her incurring the sin of Adam, before He had made on the Cross atonement for it. And therefore it is that we *preach* her who is the subject of this wonderful grace.

But she was the *Virgo Prædicanda* for another reason. When, why, what things do we preach? We preach what is not known, that it may *become* known. And hence the Apostles are said in Scripture to "preach Christ." To whom? To those who knew Him not—to the heathen world. Not to those who knew Him, but to those who did not know Him. Preaching is a gradual work: first one lesson, then another. Thus were the heathen brought into the Church gradually. And in like manner, the preaching of Mary to the children of the Church, and the devotion paid to her by them, has grown, grown gradually, with successive ages. Not so much preached about her in early times as in later. First she was preached as the Virgin of Virgins—then as the Mother of God—then as glorious in her Assumption—then as the Advocate of sinners—then as Immaculate in her Conception. And this last has been the special preaching of the present century; and thus that which was earliest in her own history is the latest in the Church's recognition of her.

I On the Immaculate Conception

MAY 5

MARY IS *THE MATER ADMIRABILIS,* THE WONDERFUL MOTHER

When Mary, the *Virgo Prædicanda*, the Virgin who is to be proclaimed aloud, is called by the title of *Admirabilis*, it is thereby suggested to us what the effect is of the preaching of her as Immaculate in her Conception. The Holy Church proclaims, preaches her, as conceived without original sin; and those who hear, the children of Holy Church, wonder, marvel, are astonished and overcome by the preaching. It is so great a prerogative.

Even created excellence is fearful to think of when it is so high as Mary's. As to the great Creator, when Moses desired to see His glory, He Himself says about Himself, "Thou canst not see My face, for man shall not see Me and live" (Exodus 33:20); and St. Paul says, "Our God is a consuming fire" (Hebrews 12:29). And when St. John, holy as he was, saw only the Human Nature of our Lord, as He is in Heaven, "he fell at His feet as dead" (Revelation 1:17). And so as regards the appearance of angels. The holy Daniel, when St. Gabriel appeared to him, "fainted away, and lay in a consternation, with his face close to the ground." When this great archangel came to Zacharias, the father of St. John the Baptist, he too "was troubled, and fear fell upon him" (Luke 1:12). But it was otherwise with Mary when the same St. Gabriel came to her. She was overcome indeed, and troubled at his words, because, humble as she was in her own opinion of herself, he addressed her as "Full of grace," and "Blessed among women;" but she was able to bear the sight of him.

Hence, we learn two things: first, how great a holiness was Mary's, seeing she could endure the presence of an angel, whose brightness smote the holy prophet Daniel even to fainting and almost to death; and secondly, since she is so much holier than that angel, and we so much less holy than Daniel, what great reason we have to call her the *Virgo Admirabilis*, the Wonderful, the Awful Virgin, when we think of her ineffable purity!

There are those who are so thoughtless, so blind, so grovelling as to think that Mary is not as much shocked at wilful sin as her Divine Son is, and that we can make her our friend and advocate, though we go to her without contrition at heart, without even the wish for true repentance and resolution to amend. As if Mary could hate sin less, and love sinners more, than our Lord does! No: she feels a sympathy for those only who wish to leave their sins; else, how should she be without sin herself? No: if even to the best of us she is, in the words of Scripture, "fair as the moon, bright as the sun, and terrible as an army set in array," what is she to the impenitent sinner?

I On the Immaculate Conception

MAY 6
MARY IS THE *DOMUS AUREA*, THE HOUSE OF GOLD

Why is she called a *House*? And why is she called *Golden*? Gold is the most beautiful, the most valuable, of all metals. Silver, copper, and steel may in their way be made good to the eye, but nothing is so rich, so splendid, as gold. We have few opportunities of seeing it in any quantity; but anyone who has seen a large number of bright gold coins knows how magnificent is the look of gold. Hence it is that in Scripture the Holy City is, by a figure of speech, called Golden. "The City," says St. John, "was pure gold, as it were transparent glass." He means of course to give us a notion of the wondrous beautifulness of heaven, by comparing it with what is the most beautiful of all the substances which we see on earth.

Therefore, it is that Mary too is called golden; because her graces, her virtues, her innocence, her purity, are of that transcendent brilliancy and dazzling perfection, so costly, so exquisite, that the angels cannot, so to say, keep their eyes off her any more than we could help gazing upon any great work of gold.

But observe further, she is a golden house, or, I will rather say, a golden palace. Let us imagine we saw a whole palace or large church all made of gold, from the foundations to the roof; such, in regard to the number, the variety, the extent of her spiritual excellences, is Mary.

But why is she called a house or palace? And whose palace? She is the house and the palace of the Great King, of God Himself. Our Lord, the Co-equal Son of God, once dwelt in her. He was her Guest; nay, more than a guest, for a guest comes into a house as well as leaves it. But our Lord was actually born in this holy house. He took His flesh and His blood from this house, from the flesh, from the veins of Mary. Rightly then was she made to be of pure gold, because she was to give of that gold to form the body of the Son of God. She was golden in her conception, golden in her birth. She went through the fire of her suffering like gold in the furnace, and when she ascended on high, she was, in the words of our hymn,

Above all the Angels in glory untold,
Standing next to the King in a vesture of gold.

I On the Immaculate Conception

MAY 7
MARY IS THE *MATER AMABILIS*, THE LOVABLE OR DEAR MOTHER

Why is she *Amabilis* thus specially? It is because she was without sin. Sin is something odious in its very nature, and grace is something bright, beautiful, attractive.

However, it may be said that sinlessness was not enough to make others love her, or to make her dear to others, and that for two reasons:

first, because we cannot like anyone that is not like ourselves, and *we* are sinners; and next, because her being holy would not make her pleasant and winning, because holy persons whom we fall in with, are not always agreeable, and we cannot like them, however we may revere them and look up to them.

Now as to the first of these two questions, we may grant that bad men do not, cannot like good men; but our Blessed Virgin Mary is called *Amabilis*, or lovable, as being such to the children of the Church, not to those outside of it, who know nothing about her; and no child of Holy Church but has some remains of God's grace in his soul which makes him sufficiently like her, however greatly wanting he may be, to allow of his being able to love her. So we may let this question pass.

But as to the second question, in other words—How are we sure that our Lady, when she was on earth, attracted people round her, and made them love her merely because she was holy?—considering that holy people sometimes have not that gift of drawing others to them.

To explain this point we must recollect that there is a vast difference between the state of a soul such as that of the Blessed Virgin, which has never sinned, and a soul, however holy, which has once had upon it Adam's sin; for, even after baptism and repentance, it suffers necessarily from the spiritual wounds which are the consequence of that sin. Holy men, indeed, never commit mortal sin; nay, sometimes have never committed even one mortal sin in the whole course of their lives. But Mary's holiness went beyond this. She never committed even a venial sin, and this special privilege is not known to belong to anyone but Mary.

Now, whatever want of amiableness, sweetness, attractiveness, really exists in holy men arises from the remains of sin in them, or again from the want of a holiness powerful enough to overcome the defects of nature, whether of soul or body; but, as to Mary, her holiness was such, that if we saw her, and heard her, we should not be able to tell to those who asked us anything about her except simply that she was angelic and heavenly.

Of course her face was most beautiful; but we should not be able to recollect whether it was beautiful or not; we should not recollect any of her features, because it was her beautiful sinless soul, which looked through her eyes, and spoke through her mouth, and was heard in her voice, and compassed her all about; when she was still, or when she walked, whether she smiled, or was sad, her sinless soul, this it was which would draw all those to her who had any grace in them, any remains of grace, any love of holy things. There was a divine music in all she said and did—in her mien, her air, her deportment, that charmed every true heart that came near her. Her innocence, her humility and modesty, her simplicity, sincerity, and truthfulness, her unselfishness, her unaffected interest in everyone who came to her, her purity—it was these qualities which made her so lovable; and were we to see her now, neither our first thought nor our second thought would be, what she could do for us with her Son (though she can do so much), but our first thought would be, "Oh, how beautiful!" and our second thought would be, "Oh, what ugly, hateful creatures are we!"

I On the Immaculate Conception

MAY 7
MARY IS THE *ROSA MYSTICA*, THE MYSTICAL ROSE
(Duplicate for the same day)

How did Mary become the *Rosa Mystica*, the choice, delicate, perfect flower of God's spiritual creation? It was by being born, nurtured and sheltered in the mystical garden or Paradise of God. Scripture makes use of the figure of a garden, when it would speak of heaven and its blessed inhabitants. A garden is a spot of ground set apart for trees and plants, all good, all various, for things that are sweet to the taste or fragrant in scent, or beautiful to look upon, or useful for nourishment; and accordingly in its spiritual sense it means the home of blessed spirits and holy souls dwelling there together, souls with both the flowers and the fruits upon them, which by the careful husbandry of God they have come to bear, flowers and fruits of grace, flowers more beautiful and more fragrant than those of any garden, fruits more delicious and exquisite than can be matured by earthly husbandman.

All that God has made speaks of its Maker; the mountains speak of His eternity; the sun of His immensity, and the winds of His Almightiness. In like manner flowers and fruits speak of His sanctity, His love, and His providence; and such as are flowers and fruits, such must be the place where they are found. That is to say, since they are found in a garden, therefore a garden has also excellences which speak of God, because it is their home. For instance, it would be out of place if we found beautiful flowers on the mountain-crag, or rich fruit in the sandy desert. As then by flowers and fruits are meant, in a mystical sense, the gifts and graces of the Holy Ghost, so by a garden is meant mystically a place of spiritual repose, stillness, peace, refreshment, and delight.

Thus, our first parents were placed in "a garden of pleasure" shaded by trees, "fair to behold and pleasant to eat of" (Genesis 2:9), with the Tree of Life in the midst, and a river to water the ground. Thus, our Lord, speaking from the cross to the penitent robber, calls the blessed place, the heaven to which He was taking him, "paradise," or a garden of pleasure. Therefore St. John, in the Apocalypse, speaks of heaven, the palace of God, as a garden or paradise, in which was the Tree of Life giving forth its fruits every month.

Such was the garden in which the Mystical Rose, the Immaculate Mary, was sheltered and nursed to be the Mother of the All Holy God, from her birth to her espousal to St. Joseph, a term of thirteen years. For three years of it she was in the arms of her holy mother, St. Anne, and then for ten years she lived in the temple of God. In those blessed gardens, as they may be called, she lived by herself, continually visited by the dew of God's grace, and growing up a more and more heavenly flower, till at the end of that period she was meet for the inhabitation in her of the Most Holy. This was the outcome of the Immaculate Conception. Excepting her, the fairest rose in the paradise of God has had upon it blight, and has had the risk of canker-worm and locust. All but Mary; she from the first was perfect in her sweetness and her beautifulness, and at length when the angel Gabriel had to come to her, he found her "full of grace," which had, from her good use of it, accumulated in her from the first moment of her being.

I On the Immaculate Conception

MAY 8
MARY IS THE *VIRGO VENERANDA*, THE ALL-WORSHIPFUL VIRGIN

We use the word *Venerable* generally of what is *old*. That is because only what is old has commonly those qualities which excite reverence or veneration.

It is a great history, a great character, a maturity of virtue, goodness, experience, that excite our reverence, and these commonly cannot belong to the young.

But this is not true when we are considering Saints. A short life with them is a long one. Thus Holy Scripture says, "Venerable age is not that of long time, nor counted by the number of years, but it is the *understanding* of a man that is gray hairs, and a spotless life is old age. The just man, if he be cut short by death, shall be at rest; being made perfect in a short time, he fulfilled a long time" (Wisdom 4:8–10).

Nay, there is a heathen writer, who knew nothing of Saints, who lays it down that even to children, to all children, a great reverence should be paid, and that on the ground of their being as yet innocent. And this is a feeling very widely felt and expressed in all countries; so much so that the sight of those who have not sinned (that is, who are not yet old enough to have fallen into mortal sin) has, on the very score of that innocent, smiling youthfulness, often disturbed and turned the plunderer or the assassin in the midst of his guilty doings, filled him with a sudden fear, and brought him, if not to repentance, at least to change of purpose.

And, to pass from the thought of the lowest to the Highest, what shall we say of the Eternal God (if we may safely speak of Him at all) but that He, because He is eternal, is ever young, without a beginning, and therefore without change, and, in the fullness and perfection of His incomprehensible attributes, now just what He was a million years ago? He is truly called in Scripture the "Ancient of Days" (Daniel 7:9), and is therefore infinitely venerable; yet He needs not old age to make him venerable; He has really nothing of those human attendants on venerableness which the sacred writers are obliged figuratively to ascribe to Him, in order to make us feel that profound abasement and reverential awe which we ought to entertain at the thought of Him.

And so of the great Mother of God, as far as a creature can be like the Creator; her ineffable purity and utter freedom from any shadow of sin, her Immaculate Conception, her ever-virginity—these her prerogatives (in spite of her extreme youth at the time when Gabriel came to her) are such as to lead us to exclaim in the prophetic words of Scripture both with awe and with exultation, "Thou art the glory of Jerusalem and the joy of Israel; thou art the honor of our people; therefore hath the hand of the Lord strengthened thee, and therefore art thou blessed forever."

I On the Immaculate Conception

MAY 9

MARY IS *SANCTA MARIA*, THE HOLY MARY

God alone can claim the attribute of holiness. Hence, we say in the Hymn, "*Tu solus sanctus*," "Thou only art holy." By holiness we mean the absence of whatever sullies, dims, and degrades a rational nature; all that is most opposite and contrary to sin and guilt.

We say that God alone is holy, though in truth all His high attributes are possessed by him in that fullness, that it may be truly said that He alone has them. Thus, as to goodness, our Lord said to the young man, "None is good but God alone." He too alone is Power, He alone is Wisdom, He alone is Providence, Love, Mercy, Justice, Truth. This is true; but holiness is singled out as His special prerogative, because it marks more than His other attributes, not only His superiority over all His creatures, but emphatically His separation from them. Hence, we read in the Book of Job, "Can man be justified compared with God, or he that is born of a woman appear clean? Behold, even the moon doth not shine, and the stars are not pure, in His sight" (Job 25:4). "Behold, among His saints none is unchangeable, and the Heavens arc not pure in His sight" (Job 15:15).

This we must receive and understand in the first place; but secondly, we know too, that, in His mercy, He has communicated in various measures His great attributes to His rational creatures, and, first of all, as being most necessary, holiness. Thus Adam, from the time of his creation, was gifted, over and above his nature as man, with the grace of God, to unite him to God, and to make him holy. Grace is therefore called holy grace; and, as being holy, it is the connecting principle between God and man. Adam in Paradise might have had knowledge, and skill, and many virtues; but these gifts did not unite him to his Creator. It was holiness that united him, for it is said by St. Paul, "Without holiness no man shall see God."

And so again, when man fell and lost this holy grace, he had various gifts still adhering to him; he might be, in a certain measure, true, merciful, loving, and just; but these virtues did not unite him to God. What he needed was holiness; and therefore, the first act of God's goodness to us in the Gospel is to take us out of our *un*holy state by means of the sacrament of Baptism, and by the grace then given us to re-open the communications, so long closed, between the soul and heaven.

We see then the force of our Lady's title, when we call her *Holy* Mary. When God would prepare a human mother for His Son, this was why He began by giving her an immaculate conception. He began, not by giving her the gift of love, or truthfulness, or gentleness, or devotion, though according to the occasion she had them all. But He began His great work before she was born; before she could think, speak, or act, by making her holy, and thereby, while on earth, a citizen of heaven. "*Tota pulchra es, Maria!*" Nothing of the deformity of sin was ever hers. Thus she differs from all saints. There have been great missionaries, confessors, bishops, doctors, pastors. They have done great works, and have taken with them numberless converts or penitents to heaven. They have suffered much, and have a superabundance of merits to show. But Mary in this way resembles her Divine Son, viz., that, as He, being God, is separate by holiness from all creatures, so she is separate from all Saints and Angels, as being "full of grace."

II On the Annunciation

MAY 10
MARY IS THE *REGINA ANGELORUM*, THE QUEEN OF ANGELS

This great title may be fitly connected with the Maternity of Mary, that is, with the coming upon her of the Holy Ghost at Nazareth after the Angel Gabriel's annunciation to her, and with the consequent birth of our Lord at Bethlehem. She, as the Mother of our Lord, comes nearer to Him than any angel; nearer even than the Seraphim who surround Him, and cry continually, "Holy, Holy, Holy."

The two Archangels who have a special office in the Gospel are St. Michael and St. Gabriel—and they both of them are associated in the history of the Incarnation with Mary: St. Gabriel, when the Holy Ghost came down upon her; and St. Michael, when the Divine Child was born.

St. Gabriel hailed her as "Full of grace," and as "Blessed among women," and announced to her that the Holy Ghost would come down upon her, and that she would bear a Son who would be the Son of the Highest.

Of St. Michael's ministry to her, on the birth of that Divine Son, we learn in the Apocalypse, written by the Apostle St. John. We know our Lord came to set up the Kingdom of Heaven among men; and hardly was He born when He was assaulted by the powers of the world who wished to destroy Him. Herod sought to take His life, but he was defeated by St. Joseph's carrying His Mother and Him off into Egypt. But St. John in the Apocalypse tells us that Michael and his angels were the real guardians of Mother and Child, then and on other occasions. First, St. John saw in vision "a great sign in heaven" (meaning by "heaven" the Church, or Kingdom of God), "a woman clothed with the sun, and with the moon under her feet, and on her head a crown of twelve stars" (Revelation 12:1); and when she was about to be delivered of her Child there appeared "a great red dragon," that is, the evil spirit, ready "to devour her son" when He should be born. The Son was preserved by His own Divine power, but next the evil spirit persecuted her; St. Michael, however, and his angels came to the rescue and prevailed against him. "There was a great battle," says the sacred writer; "Michael and his Angels fought with the dragon, and the dragon fought and his angels; and that great dragon was cast out, the old serpent, who is called the devil" (Revelation 12:7). Now, as then, the Blessed Mother of God has hosts of angels who do her service; and she is their Queen.

II On the Annunciation

MAY 11
MARY IS THE *SPECULUM JUSTITIÆ*, THE MIRROR OF JUSTICE

Here first we must consider what is meant by justice, for the word as used by the Church has not that sense which it bears in ordinary English. By "justice" is not meant the virtue of fairness, equity, uprightness in our dealings; but it is a word denoting all virtues at once, a perfect, virtuous state of soul—righteousness, or moral perfection; so that it answers very nearly to what is meant by sanctity. Therefore, when our Lady is called the "Mirror of Justice," it is meant to say that she is the Mirror of sanctity, holiness, supernatural goodness.

Next, what is meant by calling her a mirror? A mirror is a surface which reflects, as still water, polished steel, or a looking-glass. What did Mary reflect? She reflected our Lord—but He is infinite Sanctity. She then, as far as a creature could, reflected His Divine sanctity, and therefore she is the Mirror of Sanctity, or, as the Litany says, of Justice.

Do we ask how she came to reflect His Sanctity?—it was by living with Him. We see every day how like people get to each other who live with those they love. When they live with those whom they don't love, as, for instance, the members of a family who quarrel with each other, then the longer they live together the more unlike each other they become; but when they love each other, as husband and wife, parents and children, brothers with brothers or sisters, friends with friends, then in course of time they get surprisingly like each other. All of us perceive this; we are witnesses to it with our own eyes and ears— in the expression of their features, in their voice, in their walk, in their language, even in their handwriting, they become like each other; and so, with regard to their minds, as in their opinions, their tastes, their pursuits. And again, doubtless in the state of their souls, which we do not see, whether for good or for bad.

Now, consider that Mary loved her Divine Son with an unutterable love; and consider too she had Him all to herself for thirty years. Do we not see that, as she was full of grace before she conceived Him in her womb, she must have had a vast, incomprehensible sanctity when she had lived close to God for thirty years?—a sanctity of an angelical order, reflecting back the attributes of God with a fullness and exactness of which no saint upon earth, or hermit, or holy virgin, can even remind us. Truly then she is the *Speculum Justitiæ*, the Mirror of Divine Perfection.

II On the Annunciation

MAY 12
MARY IS THE *SEDES SAPIENTIÆ*, THE SEAT OF WISDOM

Mary has this title in her Litany, because the Son of God, who is also called in Scripture the Word and Wisdom of God, once dwelt in her, and then, after His birth of her, was carried in her arms and seated in her lap in His first years. Thus, being, as it were, the human throne of Him who reigns in heaven, she is called the Seat of Wisdom. In the poet's words:

His throne, thy bosom blest,
O Mother undefiled,
That Throne, if aught beneath the skies,
Beseems the sinless Child.

But the possession of her Son lasted beyond His infancy—He was under her rule, as St. Luke tells us, and lived with her in her house, till He went forth to preach—that is, for at least a whole thirty years. And this brings us to a reflection about her, cognate to that which was suggested to us yesterday by the title of "Mirror of Justice." For if such close and continued intimacy with her Son created in her a sanctity inconceivably great, must not also the knowledge which she gained during those many years from His conversation of present, past, and future, have been so large, and so profound, and so diversified, and so thorough, that, though she was a poor woman without human advantages, she must in her knowledge of creation, of the universe, and of history, have excelled the greatest of philosophers, and in her theological knowledge the greatest of theologians, and in her prophetic discernment the most favored of prophets?

What was the grand theme of conversation between her and her Son but the nature, the attributes, the providence, and the works of Almighty God? Would not our Lord be ever glorifying the Father who sent Him? Would He not unfold to her the solemn eternal decrees, and the purposes and will of God? Would He not from time to time enlighten her in all those points of doctrine which have been first discussed and then settled in the Church from the time of the Apostles till now, and all that shall be till the end—nay, these, and far more than these? All that is obscure, all that is fragmentary in revelation, would, so far as the knowledge is possible to man, be brought out to her in clearness and simplicity by Him who is the Light of the World.

And so, of the events which are to come. God spoke to the Prophets: we have His communications to them in Scripture. But He spoke to them in figure and parable. There was one, in other words, Moses, to whom He vouchsafed to speak face to face. "If there be among you a prophet of the Lord," God says, "I will appear to him in a vision, and I will speak to him in a dream. But it is not so with my servant Moses. . . . For I will speak to him mouth to mouth, and plainly, and not by riddles and figures doth he see the Lord" (Numbers 12:6–8). This was the great privilege of the inspired Lawgiver of the Jews; but how much was it below that of Mary! Moses had the privilege only now and then, from time to time; but Mary for thirty continuous years saw and heard Him, being all through that time face to face with Him, and being able to ask Him any question which she wished explained, and knowing that the answers she received were from the Eternal God, who neither deceives nor can be deceived.

II On the Annunciation

MAY 13
MARY IS THE *JANUA CŒLI*, THE GATE OF HEAVEN

Mary is called the Gate of Heaven, because it was through her that our Lord passed from heaven to earth. The Prophet Ezekiel, prophesying of Mary, says, "the gate shall be closed, it shall not be opened, and no man shall pass through it, since the Lord God of Israel has entered through it—and it shall be closed for the Prince, the Prince Himself shall sit in it" (Ezekiel 44:2).

Now this is fulfilled, not only in our Lord having taken·flesh from her, and being her Son, but, moreover, in that she had a place in the economy of Redemption; it is fulfilled in her spirit and will, as well as in her body. Eve had a part in the fall of man, though it was Adam who was our representative, and whose sin made us sinners. It was Eve who began, and who tempted Adam. Scripture says: "The woman saw that the tree was good to eat, and fair to the eyes, and delightful to behold; and she took of the fruit thereof, and did eat, and gave to her husband, and he did eat." It was fitting then in God's mercy that, as the woman began the destruction of the world, so woman should also begin its recovery, and that, as Eve opened the way for the fatal deed of the first Adam, so Mary should open the way for the great achievement of the second Adam, even our Lord Jesus Christ, who came to save the world by dying on the cross for it. Hence Mary is called by the holy Fathers a second and a better Eve, as having taken that first step in the salvation of mankind which Eve took in its ruin.

How, and when, did Mary take part, and the initial part, in the world's restoration? It was when the Angel Gabriel came to her to announce to her the great dignity which was to be her portion. St. Paul bids us "present our bodies to God as a reasonable service" (Romans 12:1). We must not only pray with our lips, and fast, and do outward penance, and be chaste in our bodies; but we must be obedient, and pure in our minds. And so, as regards the Blessed Virgin, it was God's will that she should undertake willingly and with full understanding to be the Mother of our Lord, and not to be a mere passive instrument whose maternity would have no merit and no reward. The higher our gifts, the heavier our duties. It was no light lot to be so intimately near to the Redeemer of men, as she experienced afterwards when she suffered with him. Therefore, weighing well the Angel's words before giving her answer to them—first she asked whether so great an office would be a forfeiture of that Virginity which she had vowed. When the Angel told her no, then, with the full consent of a full heart, full of God's love to her and her own lowliness, she said, "Behold the handmaid of the Lord; be it done unto me according to thy word." It was by this consent that she became the Gate of Heaven.

II On the Annunciation

MAY 14
MARY IS THE *MATER CREATORIS,*
THE MOTHER OF THE CREATOR

This is a title which, of all others, we should have thought it impossible for any creature to possess. At first sight we might be tempted to say that it throws into confusion our primary ideas of the Creator and the creature, the Eternal and the temporal, the Self-subsisting and the dependent; and yet on further consideration we shall see that we cannot refuse the title to Mary without denying the Divine Incarnation—that is, the great and fundamental truth of revelation, that God became man.

And this was seen from the first age of the Church. Christians were accustomed from the first to call the Blessed Virgin "The Mother of God," because they saw that it was impossible to deny her that title without denying St. John's words, "The Word" (that is, God the Son) "was made flesh" (John 1:1).

And in no long time it was found necessary to proclaim this truth by the voice of an Ecumenical Council of the Church. For, in consequence of the dislike which men have of a mystery, the error sprang up that our Lord was not really God, but a man, differing from us in this merely—that God dwelt in Him, as God dwells in all good men, only in a higher measure; as the Holy Spirit dwelt in Angels and Prophets, as in a sort of Temple; or again, as our Lord now dwells in the Tabernacle in church. And then the bishops and faithful people found there was no other way of hindering this false, bad view being taught but by declaring distinctly, and making it a point of faith, that Mary was the Mother, not of man only, but of God. And since that time the title of Mary, as Mother of God, has become what is called a dogma, or article of faith, in the Church.

But this leads us to a larger view of the subject. Is this title as given to Mary more wonderful than the doctrine that God, without ceasing to be God, should become man? Is it more mysterious that Mary should be Mother of God, than that God should be man? Yet the latter, as I have said, is the elementary truth of revelation, witnessed by Prophets, Evangelists, and Apostles all through Scripture. And what can be more consoling and joyful than the wonderful promises which follow from this truth, that Mary is the Mother of God?— the great wonder, namely, that we become the brethren of our God; that, if we live well, and die in the grace of God, we shall all of us hereafter be taken up by our Incarnate God to that place where angels dwell; that our bodies shall be raised from the dust, and be taken to Heaven; that we shall be really united to God; that we shall be partakers of the Divine nature; that each of us, soul and body, shall be plunged into the abyss of glory which surrounds the Almighty; that we shall see Him, and share His blessedness, according to the text, "Whosoever shall do the will of My Father that is in Heaven, the same is My brother, and sister, and mother" (Matthew 12:50).

II On the Annunciation

MAY 15

MARY IS THE *MATER CHRISTI*, THE MOTHER OF CHRIST

Each of the titles of Mary has its own special meaning and drift, and may be made the subject of a distinct meditation. She is invoked by us as the Mother of Christ. What is the force of thus addressing her? It is to bring before us that she it is whom from the first was prophesied of, and associated with the hopes and prayers of all holy men, of all true worshippers of God, of all who "looked for the redemption of Israel" in every age before that redemption came.

Our Lord was called the Christ, or the Messiah, by the Jewish prophets and the Jewish people. The two words *Christ* and *Messiah* mean the same. They mean in English the "Anointed." In the old time, there were three great ministries or offices by means of which God spoke to His chosen people, the Israelites, or, as they were afterward called, the Jews, namely, that of Priest, that of King, and that of Prophet. Those who were chosen by God for one or other of these offices were solemnly anointed with oil—oil signifying the grace of God, which was given to them for the due performance of their high duties. But our Lord was all three, a Priest, a Prophet, and a King—a Priest, because He offered Himself as a sacrifice for our sins; a Prophet, because He revealed to us the Holy Law of God; and a King, because He rules over us. Thus, He is the one true Christ.

It was in expectation of this great Messiah that the chosen people, the Jews, or Israelites, or Hebrews (for these are different names for the same people), looked out from age to age. He was to come to set all things right. And next to this great question which occupied their minds, namely, When was He to come, was the question, Who was to be His Mother? It had been told them from the first, not that He should come from heaven, but that He should be born of a Woman. At the time of the fall of Adam, God had said that the seed of the Woman should bruise the Serpent's head. Who, then, was to be that Woman thus significantly pointed out to the fallen race of Adam? At the end of many centuries, it was further revealed to the Jews that the great *Messias*, or Christ, the seed of the Woman, should be born of their race, and of one particular tribe of the twelve tribes into which that race was divided. From that time, every woman of that tribe hoped to have the great privilege of herself being the Mother of the Messiah, or Christ; for it stood to reason, since He was so great, the Mother must be great, and good, and blessed too. Hence it was, among other reasons, that they thought so highly of the marriage state, because, not knowing the mystery of the miraculous conception of the Christ when He was actually to come, they thought that the marriage rite was the ordinance necessary for His coming.

Hence it was, if Mary had been as other women, she would have longed for marriage, as opening on her the prospect of bearing the great King. But she was too humble and too pure for such thoughts. She had been inspired to choose that better way of serving God which had not been made known to the Jews—the state of Virginity. She preferred to be His Spouse to being His Mother. Accordingly, when the Angel Gabriel announced to her her high destiny, she shrank from it till she was assured that it would not oblige her to revoke her purpose of a virgin life devoted to her God.

Thus, was it that she became the Mother of the Christ, not in that way which pious women for so many ages had expected Him, but, declining the grace of such maternity, she gained it by means of a higher grace. And this is the full meaning of St. Elizabeth's words, when the Blessed Virgin came to visit her, which we use in the Hail Mary: "Blessed art thou among women, and blessed is the fruit of thy womb" (Luke 1:42). And therefore, it is that in the Devotion called the "Crown of Twelve Stars" we give praise to God the Holy Ghost, through whom she was both Virgin and Mother.

II On the Annunciation

MAY 16
MARY IS THE *MATER SALVATORIS*, THE MOTHER OF THE SAVIOR

Here again, as in our reflections of yesterday, we must understand what is meant by calling our Lord a Savior, in order to understand why it is used to form one of the titles given to Mary in her Litany.

The special name by which our Lord was known before His coming was, as we found yesterday, that of Messiah, or Christ. Thus, He was known to the Jews. But when He actually showed Himself on earth, He was known by three new titles, the Son of God, the Son of Man, and the Savior; the first expressive of His Divine Nature, the second of His Human, the third of His Personal Office. Thus, the Angel who appeared to Mary called Him the Son of God; the angel who appeared to Joseph called Him Jesus, which means in English, Savior; and so the Angels, too, called Him a Savior when they appeared to the shepherds. But He Himself specially calls Himself the Son of Man.

Not Angels only call Him Savior, but those two greatest of the Apostles, St. Peter and St. Paul, in their first preachings. St. Peter says He is "a Prince and a Savior," and St. Paul says, "a Savior, Jesus." And both Angels and Apostles tell us why He is so called—because He has rescued us from the power of the evil spirit, and from the guilt and misery of our sins. Thus, the Angel says to Joseph, "Thou shalt call His name Jesus, for He shall save His people from their sins" (Matthew 1:21); and St. Peter, "God has exalted Him to be Prince and Savior, to give repentance to Israel, and remission of sins" (Acts 5:31). And He says Himself, "The Son of Man is come to seek and to save that which is lost" (Luke 19:10).

Now let us consider how this affects our thoughts of Mary. To rescue slaves from the power of the Enemy implies a conflict. Our

Lord, because He was a Savior, was a warrior. He could not deliver the captives without a fight, nor without personal suffering. Now, who are they who especially hate wars? A heathen poet answers. "Wars," he says, "are hated by Mothers." Mothers are just those who especially suffer in a war. They may glory in the honor gained by their children; but still such glorying does not wipe out one particle of the long pain, the anxiety, the suspense, the desolation, and the anguish which the mother of a soldier feels. So it was with Mary. For thirty years, she was blessed with the continual presence of her Son—nay, she had Him in subjection. But the time came when that war called for Him for which He had come upon earth. Certainly, He came, not simply to be the Son of Mary, but to be the Savior of Man, and therefore at length He parted from her. She knew then what it was to be the mother of a soldier. He left her side; she saw Him no longer; she tried in vain to get near Him. He had for years lived in her embrace, and after that, at least in her dwelling—but now, in His own words, "The Son of Man had not where to lay His head." And then, when years had run out, she heard of His arrest, His mock trial, and His passion. At last she got near Him—when and where?—on the way to Calvary: and when He had been lifted upon the Cross. And at length she held Him again in her arms: yes—when He was dead. True, He rose from the dead; but still she did not thereby gain Him, for He ascended on high, and she did not at once follow Him. No, she remained on earth many years—in the care, indeed, of His dearest Apostle, St. John. But what was even the holiest of men compared with her own Son, and Him the Son of God? O Holy Mary, Mother of our Savior, in this meditation we have now suddenly passed from the Joyful Mysteries to the Sorrowful, from Gabriel's Annunciation to thee, to the Seven Dolours.[3] That, then, will be the next series of Meditations which we make about thee.

---

3   For twenty-first-century readers: "Dolours" means Sorrows.

III Our Lady's Dolours

MAY 17
MARY IS THE *REGINA MARTYRUM*, THE QUEEN OF MARTYRS

Why is she so called?—she who never had any blow, or wound, or other injury to her consecrated person. How can she be exalted over those whose bodies suffered the most ruthless violence and the keenest torments for our Lord's sake? She is, indeed, Queen of all Saints, of those who "walk with Christ in white, for they are worthy;" but how of those "who were slain for the Word of God, and for the testimony which they held?"

To answer this question, it must be recollected that the pains of the soul may be as fierce as those of the body. Bad men who are now in hell, and the elect of God who are in purgatory, are suffering only in their souls, for their bodies are still in the dust; yet how severe is that suffering! And perhaps most people who have lived long can bear witness in their own persons to a sharpness of distress which was like a sword cutting them, to a weight and force of sorrow which seemed to throw them down, though bodily pain there was none.

What an overwhelming horror it must have been for the Blessed Mary to witness the Passion and the Crucifixion of her Son! Her anguish was, as Holy Simeon had announced to her, at the time of that Son's Presentation in the Temple, a sword piercing her soul. If our Lord Himself could not bear the prospect of what was before Him, and was covered in the thought of it with a bloody sweat, His soul thus acting upon His body, does not this show how great mental pain can be? and would it have been wonderful though Mary's head and heart had given way as she stood under His Cross?

Thus, is she most truly the Queen of Martyrs.

III Our Lady's Dolours

MAY 18

MARY IS THE *VAS INSIGNE* DEVOTIONIS, THE MOST DEVOUT VIRGIN

To be devout is to be devoted. We know what is meant by a devoted wife or daughter. It is one whose thoughts center in the person so deeply loved, so tenderly cherished. She follows him about with her eyes; she is ever seeking some means of serving him; and, if her services are very small in their character, that only shows how intimate they are, and how incessant. And especially if the object of her love be weak, or in pain, or near to die, still more intensely does she live in his life, and know nothing but him.

This intense devotion towards our Lord, forgetting self in love for Him, is instanced in St. Paul, who says. "I know nothing but Jesus Christ and Him crucified." And again, "I live, [yet] now not I, but Christ liveth in me; and [the life] that I now live in the flesh, I live in the faith of the Son of God, who loved me, and delivered Himself for me" (Galatians 2:19–20).

But great as was St. Paul's devotion to our Lord, much greater was that of the Blessed Virgin; because she was His Mother, and because she had Him and all His sufferings actually before her eyes, and because she had the long intimacy of thirty years with Him, and because she was from her special sanctity so ineffably near to Him in spirit. When, then, He was mocked, bruised, scourged, and nailed to the Cross, she felt as keenly as if every indignity and torture inflicted on Him was struck at herself. She could have cried out in agony at every pang of His.

This is called her compassion, or her suffering with her Son, and it arose from this that she was the *Vas insigne devotionis*.

MAY 19
MARY IS THE *VAS HONORABILE,* THE VESSEL OF HONOR

St. Paul calls elect souls vessels of honor: of honor, because they are elect or chosen; and vessels, because, through the love of God, they are filled with God's heavenly and holy grace. How much more then is Mary a vessel of honor by reason of her having within her, not only the grace of God, but the very Son of God, formed as regards His flesh and blood out of her!

But this title *honorabile,* as applied to Mary, admits of a further and special meaning. She was a martyr without the rude dishonor which accompanied the sufferings of martyrs. The martyrs were seized, haled about, thrust into prison with the vilest criminals, and assailed with the most blasphemous words and foulest speeches which Satan could inspire. Nay, such was the unutterable trial also of the holy women, young ladies, the spouses of Christ, whom the heathen seized, tortured, and put to death. Above all, our Lord Himself, whose sanctity was greater than any created excellence or vessel of grace—even He, as we know well, was buffeted, stripped, scourged, mocked, dragged about, and then stretched, nailed, lifted up on a high cross, to the gaze of a brutal multitude.

But He, who bore the sinner's shame for sinners, spared His Mother, who was sinless, this supreme indignity. Not in the body, but in the soul, she suffered. True, in His Agony she was agonized; in His Passion she suffered a fellow-passion; she was crucified with Him; the spear that pierced His breast pierced through her spirit. Yet there were no visible signs of this intimate martyrdom; she stood up, still, collected, motionless, solitary, under the Cross of her Son, surrounded by Angels, and shrouded in her virginal sanctity from the notice of all who were taking part in His Crucifixion.

III Our Lady's Dolours

MAY 20

MARY IS THE *VAS SPIRITUALE*, THE SPIRITUAL VESSEL

To be spiritual is to live in the world of spirits—as St. Paul says, "Our conversation is in Heaven" (Philippians 3:20). To be spiritually-minded is to see by faith all those good and holy beings who actually surround us, though we see them not with our bodily eyes; to see them by faith as vividly as we see the things of earth—the green country, the blue sky, and the brilliant sunshine. Hence it is that, when saintly souls are favored with heavenly visions, these visions are but the extraordinary continuations and the crown, by a divine intuition, of objects which, by the ordinary operation of grace, are ever before their minds.

These visions consoled and strengthened the Blessed Virgin in all her sorrows. The Angels who were around her understood her, and she understood them, with a directness which is not to be expected in their intercourse with us who have inherited from Adam the taint of sin. Doubtless; but still let us never forget that as she in her sorrows was comforted by Angels, so it is our privilege in the many trials of life to be comforted, in our degree, by the same heavenly messengers of the Most High; nay, by Almighty God Himself, the third Person of the Holy Trinity, who has taken on Himself the office of being our Paraclete, or Present Help.

Let all those who are in trouble take this comfort to themselves, if they are trying to lead a spiritual life. If they call on God, He will answer them. Though they have no earthly friend, they have Him, who, as He felt for His Mother when He was on the Cross, now that He is in His glory feels for the lowest and feeblest of His people.

III Our Lady's Dolours

MAY 21

MARY IS THE *CONSOLATRIX AFFLICTORUM*, THE CONSOLER OF THE AFFLICTED

St. Paul says that his Lord comforted him in all his tribulations, that he also might be able to comfort them who are in distress, by the encouragement which he received from God. This is the secret of true consolation: those are able to comfort others who, in their own case, have been much tried, and have felt the need of consolation, and have received it. So, of our Lord Himself it is said: "In that He Himself hath suffered and been tempted, He is able to succor those also that are tempted" (Hebrews 2:18).

And this too is why the Blessed Virgin is the comforter of the afflicted. We all know how special a mother's consolation is, and we are allowed to call Mary our Mother from the time that our Lord from the Cross established the relation of mother and son between her and St. John. And she especially can console us because she suffered more than mothers in general. Women, at least delicate women, are commonly shielded from rude experience of the highways of the world; but she, after our Lord's Ascension, was sent out into foreign lands almost as the Apostles were, a sheep among wolves. In spite of all St. John's care of her, which was as great as was St. Joseph's in her younger days, she, more than all the saints of God, was a stranger and a pilgrim upon earth, in proportion to her greater love of Him who had been on earth, and had gone away. As, when our Lord was an Infant, she had to flee across the desert to the heathen Egypt, so, when He had ascended on high, she had to go on shipboard to the heathen Ephesus, where she lived and died.

O ye who are in the midst of rude neighbors or scoffing companions, or of wicked acquaintance, or of spiteful enemies, and are helpless, invoke the aid of Mary by the memory of her own sufferings among the heathen Greeks and the heathen Egyptians.

III Our Lady's Dolours

MAY 22

MARY IS THE *VIRGO PRUDENTISSIMA*, THE MOST PRUDENT VIRGIN

It may not appear at first sight how the virtue of prudence is connected with the trials and sorrows of our Lady's life; yet there is a point of view from which we are reminded of her prudence by those trials. It must be recollected that she is not only the great instance of the contemplative life, but also of the practical; and the practical life is at once a life of penance and of prudence, if it is to be well discharged. Now Mary was as full of external work and hard service as any Sister of Charity at this day. Of course, her duties varied according to the seasons of her life, as a young maiden, as a wife, as a mother, and as a widow; but still her life was full of duties day by day and hour by hour. As a stranger in Egypt, she had duties towards the poor heathen among whom she was thrown. As a dweller in Nazareth, she had her duties towards her kinsfolk and neighbors. She had her duties, though unrecorded, during those years in which our Lord was preaching and proclaiming His Kingdom. After He had left this earth, she had her duties towards the Apostles, and especially towards the Evangelists. She had duties towards the Martyrs, and to the Confessors in prison; to the sick, to the ignorant, and to the poor. Afterwards, she had to seek with St. John another and a heathen country, where her happy death took place. But before that death, how much must she have suffered in her life amid an idolatrous population! Doubtless the Angels screened her eyes from the worst crimes there committed. Still, she was full of duties there—and in consequence she was full of merit. All her acts were perfect, all were the best that could be done. Now, always to be awake, guarded, fervent, so as to be able to act not only without sin, but in the best possible way, in the varying circumstances of each day, denotes a life of untiring mindfulness. But of such a life, Prudence is the presiding virtue. It is, then, through the pains and sorrows of her earthly pilgrimage that we are able to invoke her as the *Virgo prudentissima*.

III Our Lady's Dolours

MAY 23
MARY IS THE *TURRIS EBURNEA*, THE IVORY TOWER

A tower is a fabric which rises higher and more conspicuous than other objects in its neighborhood. Thus, when we say a man "towers" over his fellows, we mean to signify that they look small in comparison of him.

This quality of greatness is instanced in the Blessed Virgin. Though she suffered more keen and intimate anguish at our Lord's Passion and Crucifixion than any of the Apostles by reason of her being His Mother, yet consider how much more noble she was amid her deep distress than they were. When our Lord underwent His agony, they slept for sorrow. They could not wrestle with their deep disappointment and despondency; they could not master it; it confused, numbed, and overcame their senses. And soon after, when St. Peter was asked by bystanders whether he was not one of our Lord's disciples, he denied it.

Nor was he alone in this cowardice. The Apostles, one and all, forsook our Lord and fled, though St. John returned. Nay, still further, they even lost faith in Him, and thought all the great expectations which He had raised in them had ended in a failure. How different this even from the brave conduct of St. Mary Magdalen! and still more from that of the Virgin Mother! It is expressly noted of her that she stood by the Cross. She did not grovel in the dust, but stood upright to receive the blows, the stabs, which the long Passion of her Son inflicted upon her every moment.

In this magnanimity and generosity in suffering she is, as compared with the Apostles, fitly imaged as a Tower. But towers, it may be said, are huge, rough, heavy, obtrusive, graceless structures, for the purposes of war, not of peace; with nothing of the beautifulness, refinement, and finish which are conspicuous in Mary. It is true: therefore, she is called the Tower of Ivory, to suggest to us, by the brightness, purity, and exquisiteness of that material, how transcendent is the loveliness and the gentleness of the Mother of God.

IV On the Assumption

MAY 24
MARY IS THE *SANCTA DEI GENITRIX*, THE HOLY MOTHER OF GOD

As soon as we apprehend by faith the great fundamental truth that Mary is the Mother of God, other wonderful truths follow in its train; and one of these is that she was exempt from the ordinary lot of mortals, which is not only to die, but to become earth to earth, ashes to ashes, dust to dust. Die she must, and die she did, as her Divine Son died, for He was man; but various reasons have approved themselves to holy writers, why, although her body was for a while separated from her soul and consigned to the tomb, yet it did not remain there, but was speedily united to her soul again, and raised by our Lord to a new and eternal life of heavenly glory.

And the most obvious reason for so concluding is this—that other servants of God have been raised from the grave by the power of God, and it is not to be supposed that our Lord would have granted any such privilege to anyone else without also granting it to His own Mother.

We are told by St. Matthew, that after our Lord's death upon the Cross "the graves were opened, and many bodies of the saints that had slept"—that is, slept the sleep of death, "arose, and coming out of the tombs after His Resurrection, came into the Holy City, and appeared to many" (Matthew 27:52–53). St. Matthew says, "many bodies of the Saints"—that is, the holy Prophets, Priests, and Kings of former times—rose again in anticipation of the last day.

Can we suppose that Abraham, or David, or Isaiah, or Ezekiel, should have been thus favored, and not God's own Mother? Had she not a claim on the love of her Son to have what any others had? Was she not nearer to Him than the greatest of the Saints before her? And is it conceivable that the law of the grave should admit of relaxation in their case, and not in hers? Therefore, we confidently say that our Lord, having preserved her from sin and the consequences of sin by His Passion, lost no time in pouring out the full merits of that Passion upon her body as well as her soul.

IV On the Assumption

MAY 25
MARY IS THE *MATER INTEMERATA*, THE SINLESS MOTHER

Another consideration which has led devout minds to believe the Assumption of our Lady into heaven after her death, without waiting for the general resurrection at the last day, is furnished by the doctrine of her Immaculate Conception.

By her Immaculate Conception is meant, that not only did she never commit any sin whatever, even venial, in thought, word, or deed, but further than this, that the guilt of Adam, or what is called original sin, never was her guilt, as it is the guilt attaching to all other descendants of Adam.

By her Assumption is meant that not only her soul, but her body also, was taken up to heaven upon her death, so that there was no long period of her sleeping in the grave, as is the case with others, even great Saints, who wait for the last day for the resurrection of their bodies.

One reason for believing in our Lady's Assumption is that her Divine Son loved her too much to let her body remain in the grave. A second reason—that now before us—is this, that she was not only dear to the Lord as a mother is dear to a son, but also that she was so transcendently holy, so full, so overflowing with grace. Adam and Eve were created upright and sinless, and had a large measure of God's grace bestowed upon them; and, in consequence, their bodies would never have crumbled into dust, had they not sinned; upon which it was said to them, "Dust thou art, and unto dust thou shalt return" (Genesis 3:19). If Eve, the beautiful daughter of God, never would have become dust and ashes unless she had sinned, shall we not say that Mary, having never sinned, retained the gift which Eve by sinning lost? What had Mary done to forfeit the privilege given to our first parents in the beginning? Was her comeliness to be turned into corruption, and her fine gold to become dim, without reason assigned? Impossible. Therefore, we believe that, though she died for a short hour, as did our Lord Himself, yet, like Him, and by His Almighty power, she was raised again from the grave.

IV On the Assumption

MAY 26
MARY IS THE ROSA MYSTICA, THE MYSTICAL ROSE

Mary is the most beautiful flower that ever was seen in the spiritual world. It is by the power of God's grace that from this barren and desolate earth there have ever sprung up at all flowers of holiness and glory. And Mary is the Queen of them. She is the Queen of spiritual flowers; and therefore she is called the Rose, for the rose is fitly called of all flowers the most beautiful.

But moreover, she is the Mystical, or hidden Rose; for mystical means hidden. How is she now "hidden" from us more than are other saints? What means this singular appellation, which we apply to her specially? The answer to this question introduces us to a third reason for believing in the reunion of her sacred body to her soul, and its assumption into heaven soon after her death, instead of its lingering in the grave until the General Resurrection at the last day.

It is this: if her body was not taken into heaven, where is it? how comes it that it is hidden from us? why do we not hear of her tomb as being here or there? why are not pilgrimages made to it? why are not relics producible of her, as of the saints in general? Is it not even a natural instinct which makes us reverent towards the places where our dead are buried? We bury our great men honorably. St. Peter speaks of the sepulcher of David as known in his day, though he had died many hundred years before. When our Lord's body was taken down from the Cross, He was placed in an honorable tomb. Such too had been the honor already paid to St. John Baptist, his tomb being spoken of by St. Mark as generally known. Christians from the earliest times went from other countries to Jerusalem to see the holy places. And, when the time of persecution was over, they paid still more attention to the bodies of the Saints, as of St. Stephen, St. Mark, St. Barnabas, St. Peter, St. Paul, and other Apostles and Martyrs. These were transported to great cities, and portions of them sent to this place or that. Thus, from the first to this day it has been a great feature and characteristic of the Church to be most tender and reverent towards the bodies of the Saints. Now, if there was anyone who more than all would be preciously taken care of, it would be our Lady. Why then do we hear nothing of the Blessed Virgin's body and its separate relics? Why is she thus the hidden Rose?

Is it conceivable that they who had been so reverent and careful of the bodies of the Saints and Martyrs should neglect her—her who was the Queen of Martyrs and the Queen of Saints, who was the very Mother of our Lord? It is impossible. Why then is she thus the hidden Rose? Plainly because that sacred body is in heaven, not on earth.

IV On the Assumption

MAY 27
MARY IS THE *TURRIS DAVIDICA*, THE TOWER OF DAVID

A tower in its simplest idea is a fabric for defense against enemies. David, King of Israel, built for this purpose a notable tower; and as he is a figure or type of our Lord, so is his tower a figure denoting our Lord's Virgin Mother.

She is called the Tower of David because she had so signally fulfilled the office of defending her Divine Son from the assaults of His foes. It is customary with those who are not Catholics to fancy that the honors we pay to her interfere with the supreme worship which we pay to Him; that in Catholic teaching she eclipses Him. But this is the very reverse of the truth.

For if Mary's glory is so very great, how cannot His be greater still who is the Lord and God of Mary? He is infinitely above His Mother; and all that grace which filled her is but the overflowings and superfluities of His incomprehensible Sanctity. And history teaches us the same lesson. Look at the Protestant countries which threw off all devotion to her three centuries ago, under the notion that to put her from their thoughts would be exalting the praises of her Son. Has that consequence really followed from their profane conduct towards her? Just the reverse—the countries, Germany, Switzerland, England, which so acted, have in great measure ceased to worship Him, and have given up their belief in His Divinity while the Catholic Church, wherever she is to be found, adores Christ as true God and true Man, as firmly as ever she did; and strange indeed would it be, if it ever happened otherwise. Thus, Mary is the Tower of David.

IV On the Assumption

MAY 28
MARY IS THE *VIRGO POTENS*, THE POWERFUL VIRGIN

This great universe, which we see by day and by night, or what is called the natural world, is ruled by fixed laws, which the Creator has imposed upon it, and by those wonderful laws is made secure against any substantial injury or loss. One portion of it may conflict with another, and there may be changes in it internally; but, viewed as a whole it is adapted to stand forever. Hence the Psalmist says, "He has established the world, which shall not be moved" (Psalm 93:1).

Such is the world of nature; but there is another and still more wonderful world. There is a power which avails to alter and subdue this visible world, and to suspend and counteract its laws; that is, the world of Angels and Saints, of Holy Church and her children; and the weapon by which they master its laws is the power of prayer.

By prayer all this may be done, which naturally is impossible. Noe prayed, and God said that there never again should be a flood to drown the race of man. Moses prayed, and ten grievous plagues fell upon the land of Egypt. Josue prayed, and the sun stood still. Samuel prayed, and thunder and rain came in wheat-harvest. Elijah prayed, and brought down fire from heaven. Elisha prayed, and the dead came to life. Ezekiel prayed and the vast army of the Assyrians was smitten and perished.

This is why the Blessed Virgin is called Powerful—nay, sometimes, All-powerful, because she has, more than anyone else, more than all Angels and Saints, this great, prevailing gift of prayer. No one has access to the Almighty as His Mother has; none has merit such as hers. Her Son will deny her nothing that she asks; and herein lies her power. While she defends the Church, neither height nor depth, neither men nor evil spirits, neither great monarchs, nor craft of man, nor popular violence, can avail to harm us; for human life is short, but Mary reigns above, a Queen forever.

IV On the Assumption

MAY 29
MARY IS THE *AUXILIUM CHRISTIANORUM,* THE HELP OF CHRISTIANS

Our glorious Queen, since her Assumption on high, has been the minister of numberless services to the elect people of God upon earth, and to His Holy Church. This title of "Help of Christians" relates to those services of which the Divine Office, while recording and referring to the occasion on which it was given her, recounts five, connecting them more or less with the Rosary.

The first was on the first institution of the Devotion of the Rosary by St. Dominic, when, with the aid of the Blessed Virgin, he succeeded in arresting and overthrowing the formidable heresy of the Albigenses in the South of France.

The second was the great victory gained by the Christian fleet over the powerful Turkish Sultan, in answer to the intercession of Pope St. Pius V, and the prayers of the Associations of the Rosary all over the Christian world; in lasting memory of which wonderful mercy Pope

Pius introduced her title *Auxilium Christianorum* into her Litany; and Pope Gregory XIII, who followed him, dedicated the first Sunday in October, the day of the victory, to Our Lady of the Rosary.

The third was, in the words of the Divine Office, "the glorious victory won at Vienna, under the guardianship of the Blessed Virgin, over the most savage Sultan of the Turks, who was trampling on the necks of the Christians; in perpetual memory of which benefit Pope Innocent XI dedicated the Sunday in the Octave of her Nativity as the feast of her august Name."

The fourth instance of her aid was the victory over the innumerable force of the same Turks in Hungary on the Feast of St. Mary ad Nives [St. Mary of the Snows], in answer to the solemn supplication of the Confraternities of the Rosary; on occasion of which Popes Clement XI and Benedict XIII gave fresh honor and privilege to the Devotion of the Rosary.

And the fifth was her restoration of the Pope's temporal power, at the beginning of this century, after Napoleon the First, Emperor of the French, had taken it from the Holy See; on which occasion Pope Pius VII set apart May 24, the day of this mercy, as the Feast of the Help of Christians, for a perpetual thanksgiving.

IV On the Assumption

MAY 30

MARY IS THE *VIRGO FIDELIS*, THE MOST FAITHFUL VIRGIN

This is one of the titles of the Blessed Virgin, which is especially hers from the time of her Assumption and glorious Coronation at the right hand of her Divine Son. How it belongs to her will be plain by considering some of those other instances in which faithfulness is spoken of in Holy Scripture.

The word *faithfulness* means loyalty to a superior, or exactness in fulfilling an engagement. In the latter sense, it is applied even to Almighty God Himself who, in His great love for us, has vouchsafed to limit His own power in action by His word of promise and His covenant with His creatures. He has given His word that, if we will take Him for our portion and put ourselves into His hands, He will guide us through all trials and temptations, and bring us safe to heaven. And to encourage and inspirit us, He reminds us, in various passages of Scripture that He is the faithful God, the faithful Creator.

And so, His true saints and servants have the special title of "Faithful," as being true to Him as He is to them; as being simply obedient to his will, zealous for His honor, observant of the sacred interests which He has committed to their keeping. Thus, Abraham is called the Faithful; Moses is declared to be faithful in all his house; David, on this account, is called the "man after God's own heart" (Acts 13:22); St. Paul returns thanks that "God accounted him faithful"; and, at the last day, God will say to all those who have well employed their talents, "Well done, good and faithful servant." (Matthew 25:23)

Mary, in like manner, is pre-eminently faithful to her Lord and Son. Let no one for an instant suppose that she is not supremely zealous for His honor, or, as those who are not Catholics fancy, that to exalt her is to be unfaithful to Him. Her true servants are still more truly His. Well as she rewards her friends, she would deem him no friend, but a traitor, who preferred her to Him. As He is zealous for her honor, so is she for His. He is the Fount of grace, and all her gifts are from His goodness. O Mary, teach us ever to worship thy Son as the One Creator, and to be devout to thee as the most highly favored of creatures.

IV On the Assumption

MAY 31
MARY IS *THE STELLA MATUTINA*, THE MORNING STAR —AFTER THE DARK NIGHT, BUT ALWAYS HERALDING THE SUN

What is the nearest approach in the way of symbols, in this world of sight and sense, to represent to us the glories of that higher world which is beyond our bodily perceptions? What are the truest tokens and promises here, poor though they may be, of what one day we hope to see hereafter, as being beautiful and rare? Whatever they may be, surely the Blessed Mother of God may claim them as her own. And so it is; two of them are ascribed to her as her titles, in her Litany—the stars above, and flowers below. She is at once the *Rosa Mystica* and the *Stella Matutina*.

And of these two, both of them well suited to her, the Morning Star becomes her best, and that for three reasons.

First, the rose belongs to this earth, but the star is placed in high heaven. Mary now has no part in this nether world. No change, no violence from fire, water, earth, or air, affects the stars above; and they show themselves, ever bright and marvelous, in all regions of this globe, and to all the tribes of men.

And next, the rose has but a short life; its decay is as sure as it was graceful and fragrant in its noon. But Mary, like the stars, abides forever, as lustrous now as she was on the day of her Assumption; as pure and perfect, when her Son comes to judgment, as she is now.

Lastly, it is Mary's prerogative to be the Morning Star, which heralds in the sun. She does not shine for herself, or from herself, but she is the reflection of her and our Redeemer, and she glorifies Him.

When she appears in the darkness, we know that He is close at hand. He is Alpha and Omega, the First and the Last, the Beginning and the End. Behold He comes quickly, and His reward is with Him, to render to everyone according to his works. "Surely I come quickly. Amen. Come, Lord Jesus."

~⌐

AVE MARIS STELLA, HAIL, STAR OF THE SEA

Truly art thou a star, O Mary! Our Lord indeed Himself, Jesus Christ, He is the truest and chiefest Star, the bright and morning Star, as St. John calls Him; that Star which was foretold from the beginning as destined to rise out of Israel, and which was displayed in figure by the star which appeared to the wise men in the East. But if the wise and learned and they who teach men in justice shall shine as stars for ever and ever; if the angels of the Churches are called stars in the Hand of Christ; if He honored the apostles even in the days of their flesh by a title, calling them lights of the world; if even those angels who fell from heaven are called by the beloved disciple stars; if lastly all the saints in bliss are called stars, in that they are like stars differing from stars in glory; therefore most assuredly, without any derogation from the honor of our Lord, is Mary His mother called the Star of the Sea, and the more so because even on her head she wears a crown of twelve stars. Jesus is the Light of the world, illuminating every man who cometh into it, opening our eyes with the gift of faith, making souls luminous by His Almighty grace; and Mary is the Star, shining with the light of Jesus, fair as the moon, and special as the sun, the star of the heavens, which it is good to look upon, the star of the sea, which is welcome to the tempest-tossed, at whose smile the evil spirit flies, the passions are hushed, and peace is poured upon the soul.

Hail then, Star of the Sea, we joy in the recollection of thee. Pray for us ever at the throne of Grace; plead our cause, pray with us, present our prayers to thy Son and Lord—now and in the hour of death, Mary be thou our help.

[We have not included the short theological treatise, "Memorandum on the Immaculate Conception," nor the Litany and Novena of St. Philip, from the original edition of this work. —The Editors]

PART TWO
Meditations on the Stations of the Cross

LONGER MEDITATIONS ON EACH STATION

Begin with an Act of Contrition.

THE FIRST STATION

Jesus is condemned to death

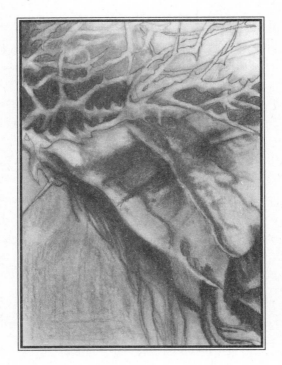

Leader: We adore Thee, O Christ, and we praise Thee.
All: Because by Thy holy cross Thou hast redeemed the world.

L eaving the House of Caiphas, and dragged before Pilate and Herod, mocked, beaten, and spit upon, His back torn with scourges, His head crowned with thorns, Jesus, who on the last day will judge the world, is Himself condemned by unjust judges to a death of ignominy and torture.

Jesus is condemned to death. His death-warrant is signed, and who signed it but I, when I committed my first mortal sins? My first mortal sins, when I fell away from the state of grace into which Thou didst place me by baptism; these it was that were Thy death-warrant, O Lord. The Innocent suffered for the guilty. Those sins of mine were the voices which cried out, "Let Him be crucified." That willingness and delight of heart with which I committed them was the consent which Pilate gave to this clamorous multitude. And the hardness of heart which followed upon them, my disgust, my despair, my proud impatience, my obstinate resolve to sin on, the love of sin which took possession of me—what were these contrary and impetuous feelings but the blows and the blasphemies with which the fierce soldiers and the populace received Thee, thus carrying out the sentence which Pilate had pronounced?

Pater, Ave, etc.

THE SECOND STATION

Jesus receives His Cross

Leader: We adore Thee, O Christ, and we praise Thee.
All: Because by Thy holy cross Thou hast redeemed the world.

A strong, and therefore heavy Cross, for it is strong enough to bear Him on it when He arrives at Calvary, is placed upon His torn shoulders. He receives it gently and meekly, nay, with gladness of heart, for it is to be the salvation of mankind.

True; but recollect, that heavy Cross is the weight of our sins. As it fell upon His neck and shoulders, it came down with a shock. Alas! what a sudden, heavy weight have I laid upon Thee, O Jesus. And, though in the calm and clear foresight of Thy mind—for Thou seest all things—Thou wast fully prepared for it, yet Thy feeble frame tottered under it when it dropped down upon Thee. Ah! how great a misery is it that I have lifted up my hand against my God. How could I ever fancy He would forgive me! unless He had Himself told us that He underwent His bitter passion in order that He might forgive us. I acknowledge, O Jesus, in the anguish and agony of my heart, that my sins it was that struck Thee on the face, that bruised Thy sacred arms, that tore Thy flesh with iron rods, that nailed Thee to the Cross, and let Thee slowly die upon it.

Pater, Ave, etc.

THE THIRD STATION

Jesus falls the first time beneath the Cross

Leader: We adore Thee, O Christ, and we praise Thee.
All: Because by Thy holy cross Thou hast redeemed the world.

Jesus, bowed down under the weight and the length of the unwieldy Cross, which trailed after Him, slowly sets forth on His way, amid the mockeries and insults of the crowd. His agony in the Garden itself was sufficient to exhaust Him; but it was only the first of a multitude of sufferings. He sets off with His whole heart, but His limbs fail Him, and He falls.

Yes, it is as I feared. Jesus, the strong and mighty Lord, has found for the moment our sins stronger than Himself. He falls—yet He bore the load for a while; He tottered, but He bore up and walked onwards. What, then, made Him give way? I say, I repeat, it is an intimation and a memory to thee, O my soul, of thy falling back into mortal sin. I repented of the sins of my youth, and went on well for a time; but at length a new temptation came, when I was off my guard, and I suddenly fell away. Then all my good habits seemed to go at once; they were like a garment which is stripped off, so quickly and utterly did grace depart from me. And at that moment I looked at my Lord, and lo! He had fallen down, and I covered my face with my hands and remained in a state of great confusion.

Pater, Ave, etc.

THE FOURTH STATION

Jesus meets His Mother

Leader: We adore Thee, O Christ, and we praise Thee.
All: Because by Thy holy cross Thou hast redeemed the world.

Jesus rises, though wounded by His fall, journeys on, with His Cross still on His shoulders. He is bent down; but at one place, looking up, He sees His Mother. For an instant they just see each other, and He goes forward.

Mary would rather have had all His sufferings herself, could that have been, than not have known what they were by ceasing to be near Him. He, too, gained a refreshment, as from some soothing and grateful breath of air, to see her sad smile amid the sights and the noises which were about Him. She had known Him beautiful and glorious, with the freshness of Divine Innocence and peace upon His countenance; now she saw Him so changed and deformed that she could scarce have recognized Him, save for the piercing, thrilling, peace-inspiring look He gave her. Still, He was now carrying the load of the world's sins, and, all-holy though He was, He carried the image of them on His very face. He looked like some outcast or outlaw who had frightful guilt upon Him. He had been made sin for us, who knew no sin; not a feature, not a limb, but spoke of guilt, of a curse, of punishment, of agony.

Oh, what a meeting of Son and Mother! Yet there was a mutual comfort, for there was a mutual sympathy. Jesus and Mary—do they forget that Passion-tide through all eternity?

Pater, Ave, etc.

THE FIFTH STATION

Simon of Cyrene helps Jesus to carry the Cross

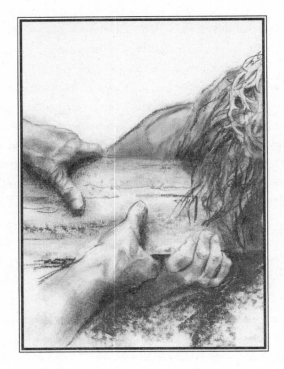

Leader: We adore Thee, O Christ, and we praise Thee.
All: Because by Thy holy cross Thou hast redeemed the world.

A t length His strength fails utterly, and He is unable to proceed. The executioners stand perplexed. What are they to do? How is He to get to Calvary? Soon they see a stranger who seems strong and active—Simon of Cyrene. They seize on him, and compel him to carry the Cross with Jesus. The sight of the Sufferer pierces the man's heart. Oh, what a privilege! O happy soul, elect of God! he takes the part assigned to him with joy.

This came of Mary's intercession. He prayed, not for Himself, except that He might drink the full chalice of suffering and do His Father's will; but she showed herself a mother by following Him with her prayers, since she could help Him in no other way. She then sent this stranger to help Him. It was she who led the soldiers to see that they might be too fierce with Him. Sweet Mother, even do the like to us. Pray for us ever, Holy Mother of God, pray for us, whatever be our cross, as we pass along on our way. Pray for us, and we shall rise again, though we have fallen. Pray for us when sorrow, anxiety, or sickness comes upon us. Pray for us when we are prostrate under the power of temptation, and send some faithful servant of thine to succor us. And in the world to come, if found worthy to expiate our sins in the fiery prison, send some good Angel to give us a season of refreshment. Pray for us, Holy Mother of God.

Pater, Ave, etc.

THE SIXTH STATION
Jesus and Veronica

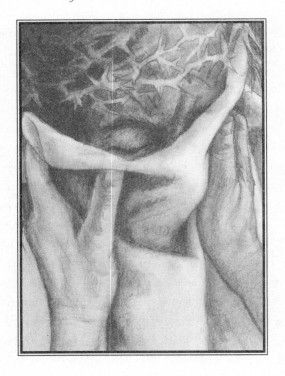

Leader: We adore Thee, O Christ, and we praise Thee.
All: Because by Thy holy cross Thou hast redeemed the world.

A s Jesus toils along up the hill, covered with the sweat of death, a woman makes her way through the crowd, and wipes His face with a napkin. In reward of her piety the cloth retains the impression of the Sacred Countenance upon it.

The relief which a Mother's tenderness secured is not yet all she did. Her prayers sent Veronica as well as Simon—Simon to do a man's work, Veronica to do the part of a woman. The devout servant of Jesus did what she could. As Magdalen had poured the ointment at the Feast, so Veronica now offered Him this napkin in His passion. "Ah," she said, "would I could do more! Why have I not the strength of Simon, to take part in the burden of the Cross? But men only can serve the Great High Priest, now that He is celebrating the solemn act of sacrifice." O Jesus! let us one and all minister to Thee according to our places and powers. And as Thou didst accept from Thy followers refreshment in Thy hour of trial, so give to us the support of Thy grace when we are hard pressed by our Foe. I feel I cannot bear up against temptations, weariness, despondency, and sin. I say to myself, what is the good of being religious? I shall fall, O my dear Savior, I shall certainly fall, unless Thou dost renew for me my vigor like the eagle's, and breathe life into me by the soothing application and the touch of the Holy Sacraments which Thou hast appointed.

Pater, Ave, etc.

THE SEVENTH STATION

Jesus falls a second time

Leader: We adore Thee, O Christ, and we praise Thee.
All: Because by Thy holy cross Thou hast redeemed the world.

The pain of His wounds and the loss of blood increasing at every step of His way, again His limbs fail Him, and He falls on the ground.

What has He done to deserve all this? This is the reward received by the long-expected Messias from the Chosen People, the Children of Israel. I know what to answer. He falls because I have fallen. I have fallen again. I know well that without Thy grace, O Lord, I could not stand; and I fancied that I had kept closely to Thy Sacraments; yet in spite of my going to Mass and to my duties, I am out of grace again. Why is it but because I have lost my devotional spirit, and have come to Thy holy ordinances in a cold, formal way, without inward affection. I became lukewarm, tepid. I thought the battle of life was over, and became secure. I had no lively faith, no sight of spiritual things. I came to church from habit, and because I thought others would observe it. I ought to be a new creature, I ought to live by faith, hope, and charity; but I thought more of this world than of the world to come—and at last I forgot that I was a servant of God, and followed the broad way that leadeth to destruction, not the narrow way which leadeth to life. And thus, I fell from Thee.

Pater, Ave, etc.

THE EIGHTH STATION

Jesus comforts the Women of Jerusalem

Leader: We adore Thee, O Christ, and we praise Thee.
All: Because by Thy holy cross Thou hast redeemed the world.

At the sight of the sufferings of Jesus the Holy Women are so pierced with grief that they cry out and bewail Him, careless what happens to them by so doing. Jesus, turning to them, said, "Daughters of Jerusalem, weep not over Me, but weep for yourselves and for your children" (Luke 23:28). Ah! can it be, O Lord, that I shall prove one of those sinful children for whom Thou biddest their mothers to weep. "Weep not for Me," He said, "for I am the Lamb of God, and am making atonement at My own will for the sins of the world. I am suffering now, but I shall triumph; and, when I triumph, those souls, for whom I am dying, will either be my dearest friends or my deadliest enemies." Is it possible? O my Lord, can I grasp the terrible thought that Thou really didst weep for me—weep for me, as Thou didst weep over Jerusalem? Is it possible that I am one of the reprobate? possible that I shall lose by Thy passion and death, not gain by it? Oh, withdraw not from me. I am in a very bad way. I have so much evil in me. I have so little of an earnest, brave spirit to set against that evil. O Lord, what will become of me? It is so difficult for me to drive away the Evil Spirit from my heart. Thou alone canst effectually cast him out.

Pater, Ave, etc.

THE NINTH STATION

Again, a third time, Jesus falls

Leader: We adore Thee, O Christ, and we praise Thee.
All: Because by Thy holy cross Thou hast redeemed the world.

Jesus had now reached almost to the top of Calvary; but, before He had gained the very spot where He was to be crucified, again He fell, and is again dragged up and goaded onwards by the brutal soldiery.

We are told in Holy Scripture of three falls of Satan, the Evil Spirit. The first was in the beginning; the second, when the Gospel and the Kingdom of Heaven were preached to the world; the third will be at the end of all things. The first is told us by St. John the Evangelist. He says: "There was a great battle in heaven. Michael and his Angels fought with the dragon, and the dragon fought, and his angels. And they prevailed not, neither was their place found any more in heaven. And that great dragon was cast out, the old serpent, who is called the devil and Satan." The second fall, at the time of the Gospel, is spoken of by our Lord when He says, "I saw Satan, like lightning, falling from heaven" (Luke 10:18). And the third by the same St. John: "There came down fire from God out of heaven, . . . and the devil . . . was cast into the pool of fire and brimstone" (Revelation 20:9,14).

These three falls—the past, the present, and the future—the Evil Spirit had in mind when he moved Judas to betray our Lord. This was just his hour. Our Lord, when He was seized, said to His enemies, "This is your hour and the power of darkness" (Luke 22:53). Satan knew his time was short, and thought he might use it to good effect. But little dreaming that he would be acting in behalf of the world's redemption, which our Lord's passion and death were to work out, in revenge, and, as he thought, in triumph, he smote Him once, he smote Him twice, he smote Him thrice, each successive time a heavier blow. The weight of the Cross, the barbarity of the soldiers and the crowd, were but his instruments. O Jesus, the only-begotten Son of God, the Word Incarnate, we praise, adore, and love Thee for Thy ineffable condescension, even to allow Thyself thus for a time to fall into the hands, and under the power of the Enemy of God and man, in order thereby to save us from being his servants and companions for eternity.

Or this,

T his is the worst fall of the three. His strength has for a while utterly failed Him, and it is some time before the barbarous soldiers can bring Him to. Ah! it was His anticipation of what was to happen to me. I get worse and worse. He sees the end from the beginning. He was thinking of me all the time He dragged Himself along, up the Hill of Calvary. He saw that I should fall again in spite of all former warnings and former assistance. He saw that I should become secure and self-confident, and that my enemy would then assail me with some new temptation, to which I never thought I should be exposed. I thought my weakness lay all on one particular side which I knew. I had not a dream that I was not strong on the other. And so, Satan came down on my unguarded side, and got the better of me from my self-trust and self-satisfaction. I was wanting in humility. I thought no harm would come on me, I thought I had outlived the danger of sinning; I thought it was an easy thing to get to heaven, and I was not watchful. It was my pride, and so I fell a third time.

Pater, Ave, etc.

THE TENTH STATION

Jesus is stripped, and drenched with gall

Leader: We adore Thee, O Christ, and we praise Thee.
All: Because by Thy holy cross Thou hast redeemed the world.

A t length, He has arrived at the place of sacrifice, and they begin to prepare Him for the Cross. His garments are torn from His bleeding body, and He, the Holy of Holiest, stands exposed to the gaze of the coarse and scoffing multitude.

O Thou who in Thy Passion wast stripped of all Thy clothes, and held up to the curiosity and mockery of the rabble, strip me of myself here and now, that in the Last Day I come not to shame before men and Angels. Thou didst endure the shame on Calvary that I might be spared the shame at the Judgment. Thou hadst nothing to be ashamed of personally, and the shame which Thou didst feel was because Thou hadst taken on Thee man's nature. When they took from Thee Thy garments, those innocent limbs of Thine were but objects of humble and loving adoration to the highest Seraphim. They stood around in speechless awe, wondering at Thy beauty, and they trembled at Thy infinite self-abasement. But I, O Lord, how shall I appear if Thou shalt hold me up hereafter to be gazed upon, stripped of that robe of grace which is Thine, and seen in my own personal life and nature? O how hideous I am in myself, even in my best estate. Even when I am cleansed from my mortal sins, what disease and corruption is seen even in my venial sins. How shall I be fit for the society of Angels, how for Thy presence, until Thou burnest this foul leprosy away in the fire of Purgatory?

Pater, Ave, etc.

THE ELEVENTH STATION

Jesus is nailed to the Cross

Leader: We adore Thee, O Christ, and we praise Thee.
All: Because by Thy holy cross Thou hast redeemed the world.

The Cross is laid on the ground, and Jesus stretched upon it, and then, swaying heavily to and fro, it is, after much exertion, jerked into the hole ready to receive it. Or, as others think, it is set upright, and Jesus is raised up and fastened to it. As the savage executioners drive in the huge nails, He offers Himself to the Eternal Father, as a ransom for the world. The blows are struck—the blood gushes forth.

Yes, they set up the Cross on high, and they placed a ladder against it, and, having stripped Him of His garments, made Him mount. With His hands feebly grasping its sides and cross-woods, and His feet slowly, uncertainly, with much effort, with many slips, mounting up, the soldiers propped Him on each side, or He would have fallen. When He reached the projection where His sacred feet were to be, He turned round with sweet modesty and gentleness towards the fierce rabble, stretching out His arms, as if He would embrace them. Then He lovingly placed the backs of His hands close against the transverse beam, waiting for the executioners to come with their sharp nails and heavy hammers to dig into the palms of His hands, and to fasten them securely to the wood. There He hung, a perplexity to the multitude, a terror to evil spirits, the wonder, the awe, yet the joy, the adoration of the Holy Angels.

Pater, Ave, etc.

THE TWELFTH STATION
Jesus dies upon the Cross

Leader: We adore Thee, O Christ, and we praise Thee.
All: Because by Thy holy cross Thou hast redeemed the world.

Jesus hung for three hours. During this time, He prayed for His murderers, promised Paradise to the penitent robber, and committed His Blessed Mother to the guardianship of St. John. Then all was finished, and He bowed His head and gave up His Spirit.

The worst is over. The Holiest is dead and departed. The most tender, the most affectionate, the holiest of the sons of men is gone. Jesus is dead, and with His death my sin shall die. I protest once for all, before men and Angels, that sin shall no more have dominion over me. This Lent I make myself God's own forever. The salvation of my soul shall be my first concern. With the aid of His grace I will create in me a deep hatred and sorrow for my past sins. I will try hard to detest sin, as much as I have ever loved it. Into God's hands I put myself, not by halves, but unreservedly. I promise Thee, O Lord, with the help of Thy grace, to keep out of the way of temptation, to avoid all occasions of sin, to turn at once from the voice of the Evil One, to be regular in my prayers, so to die to sin that Thou mayest not have died for me on the Cross in vain.

Pater, Ave, etc.

THE THIRTEENTH STATION

Jesus is taken from the Cross, and laid in Mary's Bosom

Leader: We adore Thee, O Christ, and we praise Thee.
All: Because by Thy holy cross Thou hast redeemed the world.

The multitude have gone home. Calvary is left solitary and still, except that St. John and the holy women are there. Then come Joseph of Arimathea and Nicodemus, and take down from the Cross the body of Jesus, and place it in the arms of Mary.

O Mary, at last thou hast possession of thy Son. Now, when His enemies can do no more, they leave Him in contempt to thee. As His unexpected friends perform their difficult work, thou lookest on with unspeakable thoughts. Thy heart is pierced with the sword of which Simeon spoke. O Mother most sorrowful; yet in thy sorrow there is a still greater joy. The joy in prospect nerved thee to stand by Him as He hung upon the Cross; much more now, without swooning, without trembling, thou dost receive Him to thy arms and on thy lap. Now thou art supremely happy as having Him, though He comes to thee not as He went from thee. He went from thy home, O Mother of God, in the strength and beauty of His manhood, and He comes back to thee dislocated, torn to pieces, mangled, dead. Yet, O Blessed Mary, thou art happier in this hour of woe than on the day of the marriage feast, for then He was leaving thee, and now in the future, as a Risen Savior, He will be separated from thee no more.

Pater, Ave, etc.

THE FOURTEENTH STATION

Jesus is laid in the Tomb

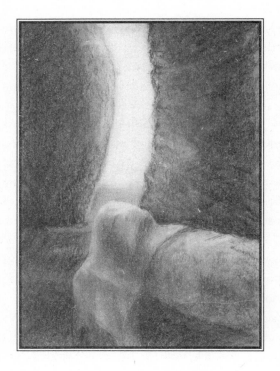

Leader: We adore Thee, O Christ, and we praise Thee.
All: Because by Thy holy cross Thou hast redeemed the world.

B ut for a short three days, for a day and a half—Mary then must give Him up. He is not yet risen. His friends and servants take Him from thee, and place Him in an honorable tomb. They close it safely, till the hour comes for His resurrection.

Lie down and sleep in peace in the calm grave for a little while, dear Lord, and then wake up for an everlasting reign. We, like the faithful women, will watch around Thee, for all our treasure, all our life, is lodged with Thee. And, when our turn comes to die, grant, sweet Lord, that we may sleep calmly too, the sleep of the just. Let us sleep peacefully for the brief interval between death and the general resurrection. Guard us from the enemy; save us from the pit. Let our friends remember us and pray for us, O dear Lord. Let Masses be said for us, so that the pains of Purgatory, so much deserved by us, and therefore so truly welcomed by us, may be over with little delay. Give us seasons of refreshment there; wrap us round with holy dreams and soothing contemplations, while we gather strength to ascend the heavens. And then let our faithful guardian Angels help us up the glorious ladder, reaching from earth to heaven, which Jacob saw in vision. And when we reach the everlasting gates, let them open upon us with the music of Angels; and let St. Peter receive us, and our Lady, the glorious Queen of Saints, embrace us, and bring us to Thee, and to Thy Eternal Father, and to Thy Co-equal Spirit, Three Persons, One God, to reign with Them for ever and ever.

Pater, Ave, etc.

Let Us Pray

God, Who by the Precious Blood of Thy only-begotten Son didst sanctify the Standard of the Cross, grant, we beseech Thee, that we who rejoice in the glory of the same Holy Cross may at all times and places rejoice in Thy protection, Through the same Christ, our Lord.

End with one Pater, Ave, and Gloria, for the intention of the Sovereign Pontiff.

SHORTER MEDITATIONS ON EACH STATION
Begin with an Act of Contrition.

FIRST STATION
Jesus condemned to Death

The Holy, Just, and True was judged by sinners, and put to death. Yet, while they judged, they were compelled to acquit Him. Judas, who betrayed Him, said, "I have sinned in that I have betrayed the innocent blood" (Matthew 27:4). Pilate, who sentenced Him, said, "I am innocent of the blood of this just person" (Matthew 27:24), and threw the guilt upon the Jews. The Centurion who saw Him crucified said, "Indeed this was a just man." Thus ever, O Lord, Thou art justified in Thy words, and dost overcome when Thou art judged. And so, much more, at the last day "They shall look on Him whom they pierced" (John 19:37); and He who was condemned in weakness shall judge the world in power, and even those who are condemned will confess their judgment is just.

THE SECOND STATION
Jesus receives His Cross

Jesus supports the whole world by His divine power, for He is God; but the weight was less heavy than was the Cross which our sins hewed out for Him. Our sins cost Him this humiliation. He had to take on Him our nature, and to appear among us as a man, and to offer up for us a great sacrifice. He had to pass a life in penance, and to endure His passion and death at the end of it. O Lord God Almighty, who dost bear the weight of the whole world without weariness, who bore the weight of all our sins, though they wearied Thee, as Thou art the Preserver of our bodies by Thy Providence, so be Thou the Savior of our souls by Thy precious blood.

THE THIRD STATION
Jesus falls under the weight of the Cross the first time

S atan fell from heaven in the beginning; by the just sentence of his Creator he fell, against whom he had rebelled. And when he had succeeded in gaining man to join him in his rebellion, and his Maker came to save him, then his brief hour of triumph came, and he made the most of it. When the Holiest had taken flesh, and was in his power, then in his revenge and malice he determined, as he himself had been struck down by the Almighty arm, to strike in turn a heavy blow at Him who struck him. Therefore, it was that Jesus fell down so suddenly. O dear Lord, by this Thy first fall raise us all out of sin, who have so miserably fallen under its power.

THE FOURTH STATION
Jesus meets His Mother

T here is no part of the history of Jesus but Mary has her part in it. There are those who profess to be His servants, who think that her work was ended when she bore Him, and after that she had nothing to do but disappear and be forgotten. But we, O Lord, Thy children of the Catholic Church, do not so think of Thy Mother. She brought the tender infant into the Temple, she lifted Him up in her arms when the wise men came to adore Him. She fled with Him to Egypt, she took Him up to Jerusalem when He was twelve years old. He lived with her at Nazareth for thirty years. She was with Him at the marriage-feast. Even when He had left her to preach, she hovered about Him. And now she shows herself as He toils along the Sacred Way with His cross on His shoulders. Sweet Mother, let us ever think of thee when we think of Jesus, and when we pray to Him, ever aid us by thy powerful intercession.

THE FIFTH STATION
Simon of Cyrene helps Jesus to carry the Cross

Jesus could bear His Cross alone, did He so will; but He permits Simon to help Him, in order to remind us that we must take part in His sufferings, and have a fellowship in His work. His merit is infinite, yet He condescends to let His people add their merit to it. The sanctity of the Blessed Virgin, the blood of the Martyrs, the prayers and penances of the Saints, the good deeds of all the faithful, take part in that work which, nevertheless, is perfect without them. He saves us by His blood, but it is through and with ourselves that He saves us. Dear Lord, teach us to suffer with Thee, make it pleasant to us to suffer for Thy sake, and sanctify all our sufferings by the merits of Thy own.

THE SIXTH STATION
The Face of Jesus is wiped by Veronica

Jesus let the pious woman carry off an impression of His Sacred Countenance, which was to last to future ages. He did this to remind us all, that His image must ever be impressed on all our hearts. Whoever we are, in whatever part of the earth, in whatever age of the world, Jesus must live in our hearts. We may differ from each other in many things, but in this we must all agree, if we are His true children. We must bear about with us the napkin of St. Veronica; we must ever meditate upon His death and resurrection, we must ever imitate His divine excellence, according to our measure. Lord, let our countenances be ever pleasing in Thy sight, not defiled with sin, but bathed and washed white in Thy precious blood.

THE SEVENTH STATION
Jesus falls a second time

Satan had a second fall, when our Lord came upon earth. By that time, he had usurped the dominion of the whole world—and he called himself its king. And he dared to take up the Holy Savior in his arms, and show Him all kingdoms, and blasphemously promise to give them to Him, His Maker, if He would adore him. Jesus answered, "Begone, Satan!" (Matthew 4:10)—and Satan fell down from the high mountain. And Jesus bare witness to it when He said, "I saw Satan, as lightning, falling from heaven" (Luke 10:18). The Evil One remembered this second defeat, and so now he smote down the Innocent Lord a second time, now that he had Him in his power. O dear Lord, teach us to suffer with Thee, and not be afraid of Satan's buffetings, when they come on us from resisting him.

THE EIGHTH STATION
The Women of Jerusalem mourn for Our Lord

Ever since the prophecy of old time, that the Savior of man was to be born of a woman of the stock of Abraham, the Jewish women had desired to bear Him. Yet, now that He was really come, how different, as the Gospel tells us, was the event from what they had expected. He said to them "that the days were coming when they should say, Blessed are the barren, and the wombs that have not borne, and the breasts which have not given suck." Ah, Lord, we know not what is good for us, and what is bad. We cannot foretell the future, nor do we know, when Thou comest to visit us, in what form Thou wilt come. And therefore, we leave it all to Thee. Do Thou Thy good pleasure to us and in us. Let us ever look at Thee, and do Thou look upon us, and give us the grace of Thy bitter Cross and Passion, and console us in Thy own way and at Thy own time.

THE NINTH STATION
Jesus falls the third time

S atan will have a third and final fall at the end of the world, when he will be shut up for good in the everlasting fiery prison. He knew this was to be his end—he has no hope, but despair only. He knew that no suffering which he could at that moment inflict upon the Savior of men would avail to rescue himself from that inevitable doom. But, in horrible rage and hatred, he determined to insult and torture while he could the great King whose throne is everlasting. Therefore, a third time he smote Him down fiercely to the earth. O Jesus, Only-begotten Son of God, the Word Incarnate, we adore with fear and trembling and deep thankfulness Thy awful humiliation, that Thou who art the Highest, should have permitted Thyself, even for one hour, to be the sport and prey of the Evil One.

THE TENTH STATION
Jesus is stripped of His Garments

J esus would give up everything of this world, before He left it. He exercised the most perfect poverty. When He left the Holy House of Nazareth, and went out to preach, He had not where to lay His head. He lived on the poorest food, and on what was given to Him by those who loved and served Him. And therefore, He chose a death in which not even His clothes were left to Him. He parted with what seemed most necessary, and even a part of Him, by the law of human nature since the fall. Grant us in like manner, O dear Lord, to care nothing for anything on earth, and to bear the loss of all things, and to endure even shame, reproach, contempt, and mockery, rather than that Thou shalt be ashamed of us at the last day.

THE ELEVENTH STATION

Jesus is nailed to the Cross

Jesus is pierced through each hand and each foot with a sharp nail. His eyes are dimmed with blood, and are closed by the swollen lids and livid brows which the blows of His executioners have caused. His mouth is filled with vinegar and gall. His head is encircled by the sharp thorns. His heart is pierced with the spear. Thus, all His senses are mortified and crucified, that He may make atonement for every kind of human sin. O Jesus, mortify and crucify us with Thee. Let us never sin by hand or foot, by eyes or mouth, or by head or heart. Let all our senses be a sacrifice to Thee; let every member sing Thy praise. Let the sacred blood which flowed from Thy five wounds anoint us with such sanctifying grace that we may die to the world, and live only to Thee.

THE TWELFTH STATION

Jesus dies upon the Cross

Consummatum est. "It is completed"—it has come to a full end. The mystery of God's love towards us is accomplished. The price is paid, and we are redeemed. The Eternal Father determined not to pardon us without a price, in order to show us especial favor. He condescended to make us valuable to Him. What we buy we put a value on. He might have saved us without a price—by the mere fiat of His will. But to show His love for us He took a price, which, if there was to be a price set upon us at all, if there was any ransom at all to be taken for the guilt of our sins, could be nothing short of the death of His Son in our nature. O my God and Father, Thou hast valued us so much as to pay the highest of all possible prices for our sinful souls—and shall we not love and choose Thee above all things as the one necessary and one only good?

THE THIRTEENTH STATION
Jesus is laid in the arms of His Blessed Mother

He is Thy property now, O Virgin Mother, once again, for He and the world have met and parted. He went out from Thee to do His Father's work—and He has done and suffered it. Satan and bad men have now no longer any claim upon Him—too long has He been in their arms. Satan took Him up aloft to the high mountain; evil men lifted Him up upon the Cross. He has not been in Thy arms, O Mother of God, since He was a child—but now thou hast a claim upon Him, when the world has done its worst. For thou art the all-favored, all-blessed, all-gracious Mother of the Highest. We rejoice in this great mystery. He has been hidden in thy womb, He has lain in thy bosom, He has been suckled at thy breasts, He has been carried in thy arms— and now that He is dead, He is placed upon thy lap. Virgin Mother of God, pray for us.

THE FOURTEENTH STATION
Jesus is laid in the Sepulcher

Jesus, when He was nearest to His everlasting triumph, seemed to be farthest from triumphing. When He was nearest upon entering upon His kingdom, and exercising all power in heaven and earth, He was lying dead in a cave of the rock. He was wrapped round in burying-clothes, and confined within a sepulcher of stone, where He was soon to have a glorified spiritual body, which could penetrate all substances, go to and fro quicker than thought, and was about to ascend on high. Make us to trust in thee, O Jesus, that Thou wilt display in us a similar providence. Make us sure, O Lord, that the greater is our distress, the nearer we are to Thee. The more men scorn us, the more Thou dost honor us. The more men insult over us, the higher Thou wilt exalt us. The more they forget us, the more Thou dost keep us in mind. The more they abandon us, the closer Thou wilt bring us to Thyself.

Let Us Pray

God, who by the Precious Blood of Thy only-begotten Son didst sanctify the standard of the Cross, grant, we beseech Thee, that we who rejoice in the glory of the same Holy Cross may at all times and places rejoice in Thy protection, through the same Christ, our Lord.

End with one Pater, Ave, and Gloria, for the intention of the Sovereign Pontiff.

MORE PRAYERS

Anima Christi

Soul of Christ, be my sanctification;
Body of Christ, be my salvation;
Blood of Christ, fill all my veins;
Water of Christ's side, wash out my stains;
Passion of Christ, my comfort be;
O good Jesu, listen to me;
In thy wounds I fain would hide,
Ne'er to be parted from Thy side;
Guard me, should the foe assail me;
Call me when my life shall fail me;
Bid me come to Thee above,
With Thy saints to sing Thy love,
  World without end. Amen.

The Heart of Mary
Written to place under a picture of the Heart of Mary.

Holy the womb that bare Him,
Holy the breasts that fed,
  But holier still the royal heart
  That in His passion bled.

Ave Maris Stella, Hail, Star of the Sea

Truly art thou a star, O Mary! Our Lord indeed Himself, Jesus Christ, He is the truest and chiefest Star, the bright and morning Star, as St. John calls Him; that Star which was foretold from the beginning as destined to rise out of Israel, and which was displayed in figure by the star which appeared to the wise men in the East. But if the wise and learned and they who teach men in justice shall shine as stars for ever and ever; if the angels of the Churches are called stars in the Hand of Christ; if He honored the apostles even in the days of their flesh by a title, calling them lights of the world; if even those angels who fell from heaven are called by the beloved disciple stars; if lastly all the saints in bliss are called stars, in that they are like stars differing from stars in glory; therefore most assuredly, without any derogation from the honor of our Lord, is Mary His mother called the Star of the Sea, and the more so because even on her head she wears a crown of twelve stars. Jesus is the Light of the world, illuminating every man who cometh into it, opening our eyes with the gift of faith, making souls luminous by His Almighty grace; and Mary is the Star, shining with the light of Jesus, fair as the moon, and special as the sun, the star of the heavens, which it is good to look upon, the star of the sea, which is welcome to the tempest-tossed, at whose smile the evil spirit flies, the passions are hushed, and peace is poured upon the soul.

Hail then, Star of the Sea, we joy in the recollection of thee. Pray for us ever at the throne of Grace; plead our cause, pray with us, present our prayers to thy Son and Lord—now and in the hour of death, Mary be thou our help.

A Triduo to St. Joseph

FIRST DAY
Consider the Glorious Titles of St. Joseph

He was the true and worthy Spouse of Mary, supplying in a visible manner the place of Mary's Invisible Spouse, the Holy Ghost. He was a virgin, and his virginity was the faithful mirror of the virginity of Mary. He was the Cherub, placed to guard the new terrestrial Paradise from the intrusion of every foe.

Blessed be the name of Joseph. Henceforth and forever. Amen.

Let us pray: God, who in Thine ineffable Providence didst vouchsafe to choose Blessed Joseph to be the husband of Thy most holy Mother, grant, we beseech Thee, that we may be made worthy to receive him for our intercessor in heaven, whom on earth we venerate as our holy Protector: who livest and reignest world without end. Amen.

SECOND DAY
Consider the Glorious Titles of St. Joseph

His was the title of father of the Son of God, because he was the Spouse of Mary, ever Virgin. He was our Lord's father, because Jesus ever yielded to him the obedience of a son. He was our Lord's father, because to him were entrusted, and by him were faithfully fulfilled, the duties of a father, in protecting Him, giving Him a home, sustaining and rearing Him, and providing Him with a trade.

Blessed be the name of Joseph. Henceforth and forever. Amen.

Let us pray: God, who in Thine ineffable Providence didst vouchsafe, etc.

THIRD DAY

Consider the Glorious Titles of St. Joseph

He is Holy Joseph, because according to the opinion of a great number of doctors, he, as well as St. John Baptist, was sanctified even before he was born. He is Holy Joseph, because his office, of being spouse and protector of Mary, specially demanded sanctity. He is Holy Joseph, because no other Saint but he lived in such and so long intimacy and familiarity with the source of all holiness, Jesus, God incarnate, and Mary, the holiest of creatures.

Blessed be the name of Joseph. Henceforth and forever. Amen.

Let us pray: God, who in Thine ineffable Providence didst vouchsafe, etc.

A Short Road to Perfection

It is the saying of holy men that, if we wish to be perfect, we have nothing more to do than to perform the ordinary duties of the day well. A short road to perfection—short, not because easy, but because pertinent and intelligible. There are no short ways to perfection, but there are sure ones.

I think this is an instruction which may be of great practical use to persons like ourselves. It is easy to have vague ideas what perfection is, which serve well enough to talk about, when we do not intend to aim at it; but as soon as a person really desires and sets about seeking it himself, he is dissatisfied with anything but what is tangible and clear, and constitutes some sort of direction towards the practice of it.

We must bear in mind what is meant by perfection. It does not mean any extraordinary service, anything out of the way, or especially heroic—not all have the opportunity of heroic acts, of sufferings—but it means what the word *perfection* ordinarily means. By perfect we mean that which has no flaw in it, that which is complete, that which is consistent, that which is sound—we mean the opposite to imperfect. As we know well what imperfection in religious service means, we know by the contrast what is meant by perfection.

He, then, is perfect who does the work of the day perfectly, and we need not go beyond this to seek for perfection. You need not go out of the round of the day.

I insist on this because I think it will simplify our views, and fix our exertions on a definite aim. If you ask me what you are to do in order to be perfect, I say, first—Do not lie in bed beyond the due time of rising; give your first thoughts to God; make a good visit to the Blessed Sacrament; say the Angelus devoutly; eat and drink to God's glory; say the Rosary well; be recollected; keep out bad thoughts; make your evening meditation well; examine yourself daily; go to bed in good time, and you are already perfect.

Prayer for the Light of Truth
I should like an enquirer to say continually:

O my God, I confess that Thou canst enlighten my darkness. I confess that Thou alone canst. I wish my darkness to be enlightened. I do not know whether Thou wilt: but that Thou canst and that I wish, are sufficient reasons for me to ask, what Thou at least hast not forbidden my asking. I hereby promise that by Thy grace which I am asking, I will embrace whatever I at length feel certain is the truth, if ever I come to be certain. And by Thy grace I will guard against all self-deceit which may lead me to take what nature would have, rather than what reason approves.

Prayer for a Happy Death

Oh, my Lord and Savior, support me in that hour in the strong arms of Thy Sacraments, and by the fresh fragrance of Thy consolations. Let the absolving words be said over me, and the holy oil sign and seal me, and Thy own Body be my food, and Thy Blood my sprinkling; and let my sweet Mother, Mary, breathe on me, and my Angel whisper peace to me, and my glorious Saints . . . smile upon me; that in them all, and through them all, I may receive the gift of perseverance, and die, as I desire to live, in Thy faith, in Thy Church, in Thy service, and in Thy love. Amen.

A Short Visit to the Blessed Sacrament
before Meditation
In the Name of the Father, and of the Son, and of the Holy Ghost.
Amen.

I place myself in the presence of Him, in whose Incarnate Presence I am before I place myself there. I adore Thee, O my Savior, present here as God and man, in soul and body, in true flesh and blood. I acknowledge and confess that I kneel before that Sacred Humanity, which was conceived in Mary's womb, and lay in Mary's bosom; which grew up to man's estate, and by the Sea of Galilee called the Twelve, wrought miracles, and spoke words of wisdom and peace; which in due season hung on the cross, lay in the tomb, rose from the dead, and now reigns in heaven. I praise, and bless, and give myself wholly to Him, who is the true Bread of my soul, and my everlasting joy.

PART THREE
Meditations on Christian Doctrine

I
HOPE IN GOD—CREATOR

1. God has created all things for good; all things for their greatest good; everything for its own good. What is the good of one is not the good of another; what makes one man happy would make another unhappy. God has determined, unless I interfere with His plan, that I should reach that which will be my greatest happiness. He looks on me individually, He calls me by my name, He knows what I can do, what I can best be, what is my greatest happiness, and He means to give it me.

2. God knows what is my greatest happiness, but I do not. There is no rule about what is happy and good; what suits one would not suit another. And the ways by which perfection is reached vary very much; the medicines necessary for our souls are very different from each other. Thus God leads us by strange ways; we know He wills our happiness, but we neither know what our happiness is, nor the way. We are blind; left to ourselves we should take the wrong way; we must leave it to Him.

3. Let us put ourselves into His hands, and not be startled though He leads us by a strange way, a *mirabilis via*, as the Church speaks. Let us be sure He will lead us right, that He will bring us to that which is, not indeed what we think best, nor what is best for another, but what is best for us.

Pray: O, my God, I will put myself without reserve into Thy hands. Wealth or woe, joy or sorrow, friends or bereavement, honor or humiliation, good report or ill report, comfort or discomfort, Thy presence or the hiding of Thy countenance, all is good if it comes from

Thee. Thou art wisdom and Thou art love—what can I desire more? Thou hast led me in Thy counsel, and with glory hast Thou received me. What have I in heaven, and apart from Thee what want I upon earth? My flesh and my heart faileth: but God is the God of my heart, and my portion forever.

4. God was all-complete, all-blessed in Himself; but it was His will to create a world for His glory. He is Almighty, and might have done all things Himself, but it has been His will to bring about His purposes by the beings He has created. We are all created to His glory—we are created to do His will. I am created to do something or to be something for which no one else is created; I have a place in God's counsels, in God's world, which no one else has; whether I be rich or poor, despised or esteemed by man, God knows me and calls me by my name.

5. God has created me to do Him some definite service; He has committed some work to me which He has not committed to another. I have my mission—I never may know it in this life, but I shall be told it in the next. Somehow, I am necessary for His purposes, as necessary in my place as an Archangel in his—if, indeed, I fail, He can raise another, as He could make the stones children of Abraham. Yet I have a part in this great work; I am a link in a chain, a bond of connection between persons. He has not created me for naught. I shall do good, I shall do His work; I shall be an angel of peace, a preacher of truth in my own place, while not intending it, if I do but keep His commandments and serve Him in my calling.

6. Therefore I will trust Him. Whatever, wherever I am, I can never be thrown away. If I am in sickness, my sickness may serve Him; in perplexity, my perplexity may serve Him; if I am in sorrow, my

sorrow may serve Him. My sickness, or perplexity, or sorrow may be necessary causes of some great end, which is quite beyond us. He does nothing in vain; He may prolong my life, He may shorten it; He knows what He is about. He may take away my friends, He may throw me among strangers, He may make me feel desolate, make my spirits sink, hide the future from me—still He knows what He is about.

Pray: O Adonai, O Ruler of Israel, Thou that guidest Joseph like a flock, O Emmanuel, O Sapientia, I give myself to Thee. I trust Thee wholly. Thou art wiser than I—more loving to me than I myself. Deign to fulfil Thy high purposes in me whatever they be—work in and through me. I am born to serve Thee, to be Thine, to be Thy instrument. Let me be Thy blind instrument. I ask not to see—I ask not to know—I ask simply to be used.

7. What mind of man can imagine the love which the Eternal Father bears towards the Only Begotten Son? It has been from everlasting—and it is infinite; so great is it that divines call the Holy Ghost by the name of that love, as if to express its infinitude and perfection. Yet reflect, O my soul, and bow down before the awful mystery, that, as the Father loves the Son, so doth the Son love thee, if thou art one of His elect; for He says expressly, "As the Father hath loved Me, I also have loved you. Abide in My love" (John 15:9). What mystery in the whole circle of revealed truths is greater than this?

8. The love which the Son bears to thee, a creature, is like that which the Father bears to the uncreated Son. O wonderful mystery! This, then, is the history of what else is so strange: that He should have taken my flesh and died for me. The former mystery anticipates the latter; that latter does but fulfill the former. Did He not love me

so inexpressibly, He would not have suffered for me. I understand now why He died for me, because He loved me as a father loves his son—not as a human father merely, but as the Eternal Father the Eternal Son. I see now the meaning of that else inexplicable humiliation: He preferred to regain me rather than to create new worlds.

9. How constant is He in His affection! He has loved us from the time of Adam. He has said from the beginning, "I will never leave thee nor forsake thee." He did not forsake us in our sin. He did not forsake me. He found me out and regained me. He made a point of it—He resolved to restore me, in spite of myself, to that blessedness which I was so obstinately set against. And now what does He ask of me, but that, as He has loved me with an everlasting love, so I should love Him in such poor measures as I can show.

Pray: O mystery of mysteries, that the ineffable love of Father to Son should be the love of the Son to us! Why was it, O Lord? What good thing didst Thou see in me a sinner? Why wast Thou set on me? "What is man, that Thou art mindful of him, and the son of man that Thou visitest him?" This poor flesh of mine, this weak sinful soul, which has no life except in Thy grace, Thou didst set Thy love upon it. Complete Thy work, O Lord, and as Thou hast loved me from the beginning, so make me to love Thee unto the end. this?

8. The love which the Son bears to thee, a creature, is like that which the Father bears to the uncreated Son. O wonderful mystery! This, then, is the history of what else is so strange: that He should have taken my flesh and died for me. The former mystery anticipates the latter; that latter does but fulfill the former. Did He not love me so inexpressibly, He would not have suffered for me. I understand now why He died for me, because He loved me as a father loves

his son—not as a human father merely, but as the Eternal Father the Eternal Son. I see now the meaning of that else inexplicable humiliation: He preferred to regain me rather than to create new worlds.

9. How constant is He in His affection! He has loved us from the time of Adam. He has said from the beginning, "I will never leave thee nor forsake thee." He did not forsake us in our sin. He did not forsake me. He found me out and regained me. He made a point of it—He resolved to restore me, in spite of myself, to that blessedness which I was so obstinately set against. And now what does He ask of me, but that, as He has loved me with an everlasting love, so I should love Him in such poor measures as I can show.

Pray: O mystery of mysteries, that the ineffable love of Father to Son should be the love of the Son to us! Why was it, O Lord? What good thing didst Thou see in me a sinner? Why wast Thou set on me? "What is man, that Thou art mindful of him, and the son of man that Thou visitest him?" This poor flesh of mine, this weak sinful soul, which has no life except in Thy grace, Thou didst set Thy love upon it. Complete Thy work, O Lord, and as Thou hast loved me from the beginning, so make me to love Thee unto the end.

II

HOPE IN GOD—REDEEMER

The Mental Sufferings of Our Lord

1. After all His discourses were consummated (Matthew 26:1), fully finished and brought to an end, then He said, The Son of man will be betrayed to crucifixion. As an army puts itself in battle array, as

sailors, before an action, clear the decks, as dying men make their will and then turn to God, so though our Lord could never cease to speak good words, did He sum up and complete His teaching, and then commence His passion. Then He removed by His own act the prohibition which kept Satan from Him, and opened the door to the agitations of His human heart, as a soldier, who is to suffer death, may drop his handkerchief himself. At once Satan came on and seized upon his brief hour.

2. An evil temper of murmuring and criticism is spread among the disciples. One was the source of it, but it seems to have been spread. The thought of His death was before Him, and He was thinking of it and His burial after it. A woman came and anointed His sacred head. The action spread a soothing tender feeling over His pure soul. It was a mute token of sympathy, and the whole house was filled with it. It was rudely broken by the harsh voice of the traitor now for the first time giving utterance to his secret heartlessness and malice. *Ut quid perditio hæc?* "To what purpose is this waste?"—the unjust steward with his impious economy making up for his own private thefts by grudging honor to his Master. Thus, in the midst of the sweet calm harmony of that feast at Bethany, there comes a jar and discord; all is wrong: sour discontent and distrust are spreading, for the devil is abroad.

3. Judas, having once shown what he was, lost no time in carrying out his malice. He went to the Chief Priests, and bargained with them to betray his Lord for a price. Our Lord saw all that took place within him; He saw Satan knocking at his heart, and admitted there and made an honored and beloved guest and an intimate. He saw him go to the Priests and heard the conversation between them. He had seen it by His foreknowledge all the time he had been about Him, and when He chose him. What we know feebly as to be, affects us

far more vividly and very differently when it actually takes place. Our Lord had at length felt, and suffered Himself to feel, the cruelty of the ingratitude of which He was the sport and victim. He had treated Judas as one of His most familiar friends. He had shown marks of the closest intimacy; He had made him the purse-keeper of Himself and His followers. He had given him the power of working miracles. He had admitted him to a knowledge of the mysteries of the kingdom of heaven. He had sent him out to preach and made him one of His own special representatives, so that the Master was judged of by the conduct of His servant. A heathen, when smitten by a friend, said, *"Et tu Brute!"* What desolation is in the sense of ingratitude! God who is met with ingratitude daily cannot from His Nature feel it. He took a human heart, that He might feel it in its fullness. And now, O my God, though in heaven, dost Thou not feel my ingratitude towards Thee?

4. I see the figure of a man, whether young or old I cannot tell. He may be fifty or he may be thirty. Sometimes He looks one, sometimes the other. There is something inexpressible about His face which I cannot solve. Perhaps, as He bears all burdens, He bears that of old age too. But so it is; His face is at once most venerable, yet most childlike, most calm, most sweet, most modest, beaming with sanctity and with loving kindness. His eyes rivet me and move my heart. His breath is all fragrant, and transports me out of myself. Oh, I will look upon that face forever, and will not cease.

5. And I see suddenly someone come to Him, and raise his hand and sharply strike Him on that heavenly face. It is a hard hand, the hand of a rude man, and perhaps has iron upon it. It could not be so sudden as to take Him by surprise who knows all things past and future, and He shows no sign of resentment, remaining calm and grave as before; but the expression of His face is marred;

a great wheal arises, and in a little time that all-gracious Face is hid from me by the effects of this indignity, as if a cloud came over It.

6. A hand was lifted up against the Face of Christ. Whose hand was that? My conscience tells me: "thou art the man." I trust it is not so with me now. But, O my soul, contemplate the awful fact. Fancy Christ before thee, and fancy thyself lifting up thy hand and striking Him! Thou wilt say, "It is impossible: I could not do so." Yes, thou hast done so. When thou didst sin willfully, then thou hast done so. He is beyond pain now: still thou hast struck Him, and had it been in the days of His flesh, He would have felt pain. Turn back in memory, and recollect the time, the day, the hour, when by willful mortal sin, by scoffing at sacred things, or by profaneness, or by dark hatred of this thy Brother, or by acts of impurity, or by deliberate rejection of God's voice, or in any other devilish way known to thee, thou hast struck The All-holy One.

Pray: O injured Lord, what can I say? I am very guilty concerning Thee, my Brother; and I shall sink in sullen despair if Thou dost not raise me. I cannot look on Thee; I shrink from Thee; I throw my arms round my face; I crouch to the earth. Satan will pull me down if Thou take not pity. It is terrible to turn to Thee; but oh turn Thou me, and so shall I be turned. It is a purgatory to endure the sight of Thee, the sight of myself—I most vile, Thou most holy. Yet make me look once more on Thee whom I have so incomprehensibly affronted, for Thy countenance is my only life, my only hope and health lies in looking on Thee whom I have pierced. So I put myself before Thee; I look on Thee again; I endure the pain in order to the purification.

O my God, how can I look Thee in the face when I think of my ingratitude, so deeply seated, so habitual, so immovable—or rather so awfully increasing! Thou loadest me day by day with Thy favors, and feedest me with Thyself, as Thou didst Judas, yet I not only do not profit thereby, but I do not even make any acknowledgment at the time. Lord, how long? when shall I be free from this real, this fatal captivity? He who made Judas his prey, has got foothold of me in my old age, and I cannot get loose. It is the same day after day. When wilt Thou give me a still greater grace than Thou hast given, the grace to profit by the graces which Thou givest? When wilt Thou give me Thy effectual grace which alone can give life and vigor to this effete, miserable, dying soul of mine? My God, I know not in what sense I can pain Thee in Thy glorified state; but I know that every fresh sin, every fresh ingratitude I now commit, was among the blows and stripes which once fell on Thee in Thy passion. O let me have as little share in those Thy past sufferings as possible. Day by day goes, and I find I have been more and more, by the new sins of each day, the cause of them. I know that at best I have a real share *in solido* of them all, but still it is shocking to find myself having a greater and greater share. Let others wound Thee—let not me. Let not me have to think that Thou wouldest have had this or that pang of soul or body the less, except for me. O my God, I am so fast in prison that I cannot get out. O Mary, pray for me. O Philip, pray for me, though I do not deserve Thy pity.

Our Lord Refuses Sympathy

1. Sympathy may be called an eternal law, for it is signified or rather transcendentally and archetypically fulfilled in the ineffable mutual love of the Divine Trinity. God, though infinitely One, has ever been Three. He ever has rejoiced in His Son and His Spirit, and they in Him—and thus through all eternity He has existed, not solitary, though alone, having in this incomprehensible multiplication of Himself and reiteration of His Person, such infinitely perfect bliss, that nothing He has created can add aught to it. The devil only is barren and lonely, shut up in himself—and his servants also.

2. When, for our sakes, the Son came on earth and took our flesh, yet He would not live without the sympathy of others. For thirty years, He lived with Mary and Joseph and thus formed a shadow of the Heavenly Trinity on earth. O the perfection of that sympathy which existed between the three! Not a look of one, but the other two understood, as expressed, better than if expressed in a thousand words—nay more than understood, accepted, echoed, corroborated. It was like three instruments absolutely in tune which all vibrate when one vibrates, and vibrate either one and the same note, or in perfect harmony.

3. The first weakening of that unison was when Joseph died. It was no jar in the sound, for to the last moment of his life, he was one with them, and the sympathy between the three only became more intense, and more sweet, while it was brought into new circumstances and had a wider range in the months of his declining, his sickness, and death. Then it was like an air ranging through a number of notes performed perfectly and exactly in time and tune by all three. But it ended in a lower note than before, and when Joseph went, a weaker one. Not that Joseph, though so saintly, added much in volume of sound to the other two, but sympathy, by its very meaning, implies number, and, on his death, one, out of three harps, was unstrung and silent.

4. O what a moment of sympathy between the three, the moment before Joseph died—they supporting and hanging over him, he looking at them and reposing in them with undivided, unreserved, supreme, devotion, for he was in the arms of God and the Mother of God. As a flame shoots up and expires, so was the ecstasy of that last moment ineffable, for each knew and thought of the reverse which was to follow on the snapping of that bond. One moment, very different, of joy, not of sorrow, was equal to it in intensity

of feeling, that of the birth of Jesus. The birth of Jesus, the death of Joseph, moments of unutterable sweetness, unparalleled in the history of mankind. St. Joseph went to limbo, to wait his time, out of God's Presence. Jesus had to preach, suffer, and die; Mary to witness His sufferings, and, even after He had risen again, to go on living without Him amid the changes of life and the heartlessness of the heathen.

5. The birth of Jesus, the death of Joseph, those moments of transcendentally pure, and perfect and living sympathy, between the three members of this earthly Trinity, were its beginning and its end. The death of Joseph, which broke it up, was the breaking up of more than itself. It was but the beginning of that change which was coming over Son and Mother. Going on now for thirty years, each of them had been preserved from the world, and had lived for each other. Now He had to go out to preach and suffer, and, as the foremost and most inevitable of His trials, and one which from first to last He voluntarily undertook, even when not imperative, He deprived Himself of the enjoyment of that intercommunion of hearts—of His heart with the heart of Mary—which had been His from the time He took man's nature, and which He had possessed in an archetypal and transcendent manner with His Father and His Spirit from all eternity.

O my soul, thou art allowed to contemplate this union of the three, and to share thyself its sympathy, by faith though not by sight. My God, I believe and know that then a communion of heavenly things was opened on earth which has never been suspended. It is my duty and my bliss to enter into it myself. It is my duty and my bliss to be in tune with that most touching music which then began to sound. Give me that grace which alone can make me hear and understand it, that it may thrill through me. Let the breathings of my soul be with Jesus, Mary, and Joseph. Let me live in obscurity, out of the world and the world's thought, with them. Let me look to them in sorrow and in joy, and live and die in their sweet sympathy.

6. The last day of the earthly intercourse between Jesus and Mary was at the marriage feast at Cana. Yet even then there was something taken from that blissful intimacy, for they no longer lived simply for each other, but showed themselves in public, and began to take their place in the dispensation which was opening. He manifested forth His glory by His first miracle; and hers also, by making her intercession the medium of it. He honored her still more, by breaking through the appointed order of things for her sake, and though His time of miracles was not come, anticipating it at her instance. While He wrought His miracle, however, He took leave of her in the words "Woman, what is between thee and Me?" Thus, He parted with her absolutely, though He parted with a blessing. It was leaving Paradise feeble and alone.

7. For in truth it was fitting that He who was to be the true High Priest, should thus, while He exercised His office for the whole race of man, be free from all human ties, and sympathies of the flesh. And one reason for His long abode at Nazareth with His Mother may have been to show, that, as He gave up His Father's and His own glory on high, to become man, so He gave up the innocent and pure joys of His earthly home, in order that He might be a Priest. So, in the old time, Melchisedech is described as without father or mother. So the Levites showed themselves truly worthy of the sacerdotal office and were made the sacerdotal tribe, because they steeled themselves against natural affection, said to father or mother, "I know you not," and raised the sword against their own kindred, when the honor of the Lord of armies demanded the sacrifice. In like manner, our Lord said to Mary, "What is between Me and thee?" It

was the setting apart of the sacrifice, the first ritual step of the Great Act which was to be solemnly performed for the salvation of the world. "What is between Me and thee, O woman?" is the offertory before the oblation of the Host. O my dear Lord, Thou who hast given up Thy mother for me, give me grace cheerfully to give up all my earthly friends and relations for Thee.

8.   The Great High Priest said to His kindred, "I know you not." Then, as He did so, we may believe that the most tender heart of Jesus looked back upon His whole time since His birth, and called before Him those former days of His infancy and childhood, when He had been with others from whom He had long been parted. Time was when St. Elizabeth and the Holy Baptist had formed part of the Holy Family. St. Elizabeth, like St. Joseph, had been removed by death, and was waiting His coming to break that bond which detained both her and St. Joseph from heaven. St. John had been cut off from his home and mankind, and the sympathies of earth, long since—and had now begun to preach the coming Savior, and was waiting and expecting His manifestation.

Pray: Give me grace, O Jesus, to live in sight of that blessed company. Let my life be spent in the presence of Thee and Thy dearest friends. Though I see them not, let not what I do see seduce me to give my heart elsewhere. Because Thou hast blessed me so much and given to me friends, let me not depend or rely or throw myself in any way upon them, but in Thee be my life, and my conversation and daily walk among those with whom Thou didst surround Thyself on earth, and dost now delight Thyself in heaven. Be my soul with Thee, and, because with Thee, with Mary and Joseph and Elizabeth and John.

9. Nor did He, as time went on, give up Mary and Joseph only. There still remained to Him invisible attendants and friends, and He had their sympathy, but them He at length gave up also. From the time of His birth we may suppose He held communion with the spirits of the Old Fathers, who had prepared His coming and prophesied of it. On one occasion, He was seen all through the night, conversing with Moses and Elias, and that conversation was about His Passion. What a field of thought is thus opened to us, of which we know how little. When He passed whole nights in prayer, it was greater refreshment to soul and body than sleep. Who could support and (so to say) re-invigorate the Divine Lord better than that "*laudabilis numerus*" of Prophets of which He was the fulfilment and antitype? Then He might talk with Abraham who saw His day, or Moses who spoke to Him; or with His especial types, David and Jeremias; or with those who spoke most of Him, as Isaias and Daniel. And here was a fund of great sympathy. When He came up to Jerusalem to suffer, He might be met in spirit by all the holy priests, who had offered sacrifices in shadow of Him; just as now the priest recalls in Mass the sacrifices of Abel, Abraham, and Melchisedech, and the fiery gift which purged the lips of Isaias, as well as holding communion with the Apostles and Martyrs.

10. Let us linger for a while with Mary—before we follow the steps of her Son, our Lord. There was an occasion when He refused leave to one who would bid his own home farewell, before he followed Him; and such was, as it seems, almost His own way with His Mother; but will He be displeased, if we one instant stop with her, though our meditation lies with Him? O Mary, we are devout to thy seven woes—but was not this, though not one of those seven, one of the greatest, and included those that followed, from thy knowledge of them beforehand? How didst thou bear that first separation from Him? How did the first days pass when thou wast

desolate? where didst thou hide thyself? where didst thou pass the long three years and more, while He was on His ministry? Once— at the beginning of it—thou didst attempt to get near Him, and then we hear nothing of thee, till we find thee standing at His cross. And then, after that great joy of seeing Him again, and the permanent consolation, never to be lost, that with Him all suffering and humiliation was over, and that never had she to weep for Him again, still she was separated from him for many years, while she lived in the flesh, surrounded by the wicked world, and in the misery of His absence.

11. The blessed Mary, among her other sorrows, suffered the loss of her Son, after He had lived under the same roof with her for thirty years. When He was no more than twelve, He gave her a token of what was to be, and said, "I must be about my Father's business" (Luke 2:49); and when the time came, and He began His miracles, He said to her, "What is to Me and to thee?" (John 2:4)—What is common to us two?—and soon He left her. Once she tried to see Him, but in vain, and could not reach Him for the crowd, and He made no effort to receive her, nor said a kind word; and then at the last, once more she tried, and she reached him in time, to see Him hanging on the cross and dying. He was only forty days on earth after His resurrection, and then He left her in old age to finish her life without Him. Compare her thirty happy years, and her time of desolation.

12. I see her in her forlorn home, while her Son and Lord was going up and down the land without a place to lay His head, suffering both because she was so desolate and He was so exposed. How dreary passed the day; and then came reports that He was in some peril or distress. She heard, perhaps, He had been led into the wilderness to be tempted. She would have shared all His sufferings, but was

not permitted. Once there was a profane report which was believed by many, that He was beside Himself, and His friends and kindred went out to get possession of Him. She went out too to see Him, and tried to reach Him. She could not for the crowd. A message came to Him to that effect, but He made no effort to receive her, nor said a kind word. She went back to her home disappointed, without the sight of Him. And so she remained, perhaps in company with those who did not believe in Him.

13 I see her too after His ascension. This, too, is a time of bereavement, but still of consolation. It was still a twilight time, but not a time of grief. The Lord was absent, but He was not on earth, He was not in suffering. Death had no power over Him. And He came to her day by day in the Blessed Sacrifice. I see the Blessed Mary at Mass, and St. John celebrating. She is waiting for the moment of her Son's Presence: now she converses with Him in the sacred rite; and what shall I say now? She receives Him, to whom once she gave birth.

Pray: O Holy Mother, stand by me now at Mass time, when Christ comes to me, as thou didst minister to Thy infant Lord—as Thou didst hang upon His words when He grew up, as Thou wast found under His cross. Stand by me, Holy Mother, that I may gain somewhat of thy purity, thy innocence, thy faith, and He may be the one object of my love and my adoration, as He was of thine.

14. There were others who more directly ministered to Him, and of whom we are told more—the Holy Angels. It was the voice of the Archangel that announced to the prophet His coming which consigned the Eternal to the womb of Mary. Angels hymned His nativity and all the Angels of God worshipped at his crib. An Angel sent Him into Egypt and brought Him back. Angels ministered to Him after His temptation. Angels wrought His miracles, when

He did not will to exert His Almighty fiat. But He bade them go at length, as He had bidden His Mother go. One remained at His agony. Afterwards He said, "Think ye not I could pray to My Father, and He would send me myriads of Angels?"—implying that in fact His guards had been withdrawn. The Church prays Him, on His ascension, "King of Glory, Lord of Angels, leave us not orphans." He, the Lord of Angels, was at this time despoiled of them.

15. He took other human friends, when He had given up His Mother—the twelve Apostles—as if He desired that in which He might sympathize. He chose them, as He says, to be, "not servants but friends" (John 15:15). He made them His confidants. He told them things which He did not tell others. It was His will to favor, nay, to indulge them, as a father behaves towards a favorite child. He made them more blessed than kings and prophets and wise men, from the things He told them. He called them "His little ones," and preferred them for His gifts to the wise and prudent. He exulted, while He praised them, that they had continued with Him in His temptations, and as if in gratitude He announced that they should sit upon twelve thrones judging the twelve tribes of Israel. He rejoiced in their sympathy when His solemn trial was approaching. He assembled them about Him at the last supper, as if they were to support Him in it. "With desire," He says, "have I desired to eat this Pasch with you, before I suffer" (Luke 22:15). Thus there was an interchange of good offices, and an intimate sympathy between them. But it was His adorable will that they too should leave Him, that He should be left to Himself. One betrayed, another denied Him, the rest ran away from Him, and left Him in the hands of His enemies. Even after He had risen, none would believe in it. Thus, he trod the winepress alone.

16. He who was Almighty, and All-blessed, and who flooded His own soul with the full glory of the vision of His Divine Nature, would still subject that soul to all the infirmities which naturally belonged to it; and, as He suffered it to rejoice in the sympathy, and to be desolate under the absence, of human friends, so, when it pleased Him, He could, and did, deprive it of the light of the presence of God. This was the last and crowning misery that He put upon it. He had in the course of His ministry fled from man to God; he had appealed to Him; He had taken refuge from the rude ingratitude of the race whom He was saving in divine communion. He retired of nights to pray. He said, "the Father loveth the Son, and shews to Him all things that He doth Himself." He returned thanks to Him for hiding His mysteries from the wise to reveal them to the little ones. But now He deprived Himself of this elementary consolation, by which He lived, and that, not in part only, but in its fullness. He said, when His passion began, "My soul is sorrowful even unto death;" and at the last, "My God, why hast Thou forsaken Me?" (Matthew 27:46). Thus He was stripped of all things.

Pray: My God and Savior, who wast thus deprived of the light of consolation, whose soul was dark, whose affections were left to thirst without the true object of them, and all this for man, take not from me the light of Thy countenance, lest I shrivel from the loss of it and perish in my infirmity. Who can sustain the loss of the Sun of the soul but Thou? Who can walk without light, or labor without the pure air, but Thy great Saints? As for me, alas, I shall turn to the creature for my comfort, if Thou wilt not give me Thyself. I shall not mourn, I shall not hunger or thirst after justice, but I shall look about for whatever is at hand, and feed on offal, or stay my appetite with husks, ashes, or chaff, which if they poison me not, at least nourish not. O my God, leave me not in that dry state in which I am; give me the comfort of Thy grace. How can I have any tenderness or sweetness, unless I have

Thee to look upon? how can I continue in prayer, as is my duty doubly, since I belong to the Oratory, unless Thou encourage me and make it pleasant to me? It is hardly that an old man keeps any warmth in him; it is slowly that he recovers what is lost. Yet, O my God, St. Philip is my father—and he seems never in his life to have been desolate. Thou didst give him trials, but didst thou ever take from him the light of Thy countenance! O Philip, wilt thou not gain for me some tithe of thy own peace and joy, thy cheerfulness, thy gentleness, and thy self-denying charity? I am in all things the most opposite to thee, yet I represent thee.

The Bodily Sufferings of Our Lord

1. His bodily pains were greater than those of any martyr, because He willed them to be greater. All pain of body depends, as to be felt at all, so to be felt in this or that degree, on the nature of the living mind which dwells in that body. Vegetables have no feeling because they have no living mind or spirit within them. Brute animals feel more or less according to the intelligence within them. Man feels more than any brute, because he has a soul; Christ's soul felt more than that of any other man, because His soul was exalted by personal union with the Word of God. Christ felt bodily pain more keenly than any other man, as much as man feels pain more keenly than any other animal.

2. It is a relief to pain to have the thoughts drawn another way. Thus, soldiers in battle often do not know when they are wounded. Again, persons in raging fevers seem to suffer a great deal; then afterwards they can but recollect general discomfort and restlessness. And so, excitement and enthusiasm are great alleviations of bodily pain; thus savages die at the stake amid torments singing songs; it is a sort of mental drunkenness. And so again, an instantaneous pain

is comparatively bearable; it is the continuance of pain which is so heavy, and if we had no memory of the pain we suffered last minute, and also suffer in the present, we should find pain easy to bear; but what makes the second pang grievous is because there has been a first pang; and what makes the third more grievous is that there has been a first and second; the pain seems to grow because it is prolonged. Now Christ suffered, not as in a delirium or in excitement, or in inadvertency, but He looked pain in the face! He offered His whole mind to it, and received it, as it were, directly into His bosom, and suffered all He suffered with a full consciousness of suffering.

3. Christ would not drink the drugged cup which was offered to Him to cloud His mind. He willed to have the full sense of pain. His soul was so intently fixed on His suffering as not to be distracted from it; and it was so active, and recollected the past and anticipated the future, and the whole passion was, as it were, concentrated on each moment of it, and all that He had suffered and all that He was to suffer lent its aid to increase what He was suffering. Yet withal His soul was so calm and sober and unexcited as to be passive, and thus to receive the full burden of the pain on it, without the power of throwing it off Him. Moreover, the sense of conscious innocence, and the knowledge that His sufferings would come to an end, might have supported Him; but He repressed the comfort and turned away His thoughts from these alleviations that He might suffer absolutely and perfectly.

Pray: O my God and Savior, who went through such sufferings for me with such lively consciousness, such precision, such recollection, and such fortitude, enable me, by Thy help, if I am brought into the power of this terrible trial, bodily pain, enable me to bear it with some portion of Thy calmness. Obtain for me this grace, O Virgin Mother, who didst see thy Son suffer and didst suffer with Him; that I, when I suffer, may associate my sufferings with His and with thine, and that through His passion, and thy merits and those of all Saints, they may be a satisfaction for my sins and procure for me eternal life.

4. Our Lord's sufferings were so great, because His soul was in suffering. What shows this is that His soul began to suffer before His bodily passion, as we see in the agony in the garden. The first anguish which came upon His body was not from without—it was not from the scourges, the thorns, or the nails, but from His soul. His soul was in such agony that He called it death: "My soul is sorrowful even unto death" (Matthew 26:38). The anguish was such that it, as it were, burst open His whole body. It was a pang affecting His heart; as in the deluge the floods of the great deep were broken up and the windows of heaven were open. The blood, rushing from his tormented heart, forced its way on every side, formed for itself a thousand new channels, filled all the pores, and at length stood forth upon His skin in thick drops, which fell heavily on the ground.

5. He remained in this living death from the time of His agony in the garden; and as His first agony was from His soul, so was His last. As the scourge and the cross did not begin His sufferings, so they did not close them. It was the agony of His soul, not of His body, which caused His death. His persecutors were surprised to hear that He was dead. How, then, did He die? That agonized, tormented heart, which at the beginning so awfully relieved itself in the rush of blood and the bursting of His pores, at length broke. It broke and He died. It would have broken at once, had He not kept it from breaking. At length, the moment came. He gave the word and His heart broke.

6. O tormented heart, it was love, and sorrow, and fear, which broke Thee. It was the sight of human sin, it was the sense of it, the feeling of it laid on Thee; it was zeal for the glory of God, horror at seeing sin so near Thee, a sickening, stifling feeling at its pollution, the deep shame and disgust and abhorrence and revolt which it inspired, keen pity for the souls whom it has drawn headlong into hell—all these feelings together Thou didst allow to rush upon Thee. Thou didst submit Thyself to their powers, and they were Thy death. That strong heart, that all-noble, all-generous, all-tender, all-pure heart was slain by sin.

Pray: O most tender and gentle Lord Jesus, when will my heart have a portion of Thy perfections? When will my hard and stony heart, my proud heart, my unbelieving, my impure heart, my narrow selfish heart, be melted and conformed to Thine? O teach me so to contemplate Thee that I may become like Thee, and to love Thee sincerely and simply as Thou hast loved me.

It is Consummated

1. It is over now, O Lord, as with Thy sufferings, so with our humiliations. We have followed Thee from Thy fasting in the wilderness till Thy death on the Cross. For forty days, we have professed to do penance. The time has been long and it has been short; but whether long or short, it is now over. It is over, and we feel a pleasure that it is over; it is a relief and a release. We thank Thee that it is over. We thank Thee for the time of sorrow, but we thank Thee more as we look forward to the time of festival. Pardon our shortcomings in Lent and reward us in Easter.

2. We have, indeed, done very little for Thee, O Lord. We recollect well our listlessness and weariness; our indisposition to mortify ourselves when we had no plea of health to stand in the way; our indisposition to pray and to meditate—our disorder of mind—our discontent, our peevishness. Yet some of us, perhaps, have done something for Thee. Look on us as a whole, O Lord, look on us as a community, and let what some have done well plead for us all.

3. O Lord, the end is come. We are conscious of our languor and lukewarmness; we do not deserve to rejoice in Easter, yet we cannot help doing so. We feel more of pleasure, we rejoice in Thee more than our past humiliation warrants us in doing; yet may that very joy be its own warrant. O be indulgent to us, for the merits of Thy own all-powerful Passion, and for the merits of Thy Saints. Accept us as Thy little flock, in the day of small things, in a fallen country, in an age when faith and love are scarce. Pity us and spare us and give us peace.

Pray: O my own Savior, now in the tomb but soon to arise, Thou hast paid the price; it is done—*consummatum est*—it is secured. O fulfill Thy resurrection in us, and as Thou hast purchased us, claim us, take possession of us, make us Thine.

III

GOD AND THE SOUL

God, the Blessedness of the Soul

1. To possess Thee, O Lover of Souls, is happiness, and the only happiness of the immortal soul! To enjoy the sight of Thee is the only happiness of eternity. At present I might amuse and sustain myself with the vanities of sense and time, but they will not last

forever. We shall be stripped of them when we pass out of this world. All shadows will one day be gone. And what shall I do then? There will be nothing left to me but the Almighty God. If I cannot take pleasure in the thought of Him, there is no one else then to take pleasure in; God and my soul will be the only two beings left in the whole world, as far as I am concerned. He will be all in all, whether I wish it or no. What a strait I shall then be in if I do not love Him, and there is then nothing else to love! if I feel averse to Him, and He is then ever looking upon me!

2. Ah, my dear Lord, how can I bear to say that Thou wilt be all in all, whether I wish it or no? Should I not wish it with my whole heart? What can give me happiness but Thou? If I had all the resources of time and sense about me, just as I have now, should I not in course of ages, nay of years, weary of them? Did this world last forever, would it be able ever to supply my soul with food? Is there any earthly thing which I do not weary of at length even now? Do old men love what young men love? Is there not constant change? I am sure then, my God, that the time would come, though it might be long in coming, when I should have exhausted all the enjoyment which the world could give. Thou alone, my dear Lord, art the food for eternity, and Thou alone. Thou only canst satisfy the soul of man. Eternity would be misery without Thee, even though Thou didst not inflict punishment. To see Thee, to gaze on Thee, to contemplate Thee, this alone is inexhaustible. Thou indeed art unchangeable, yet in Thee there are always more glorious depths and more varied attributes to search into; we shall ever be beginning as if we had never gazed upon Thee. In Thy presence are torrents of delight, which whoso tastes will never let go. This is my true portion, O my Lord, here and hereafter!

3. My God, how far am I from acting according to what I know so well! I confess it, my heart goes after shadows. I love anything better than communion with Thee. I am ever eager to get away from Thee. Often, I find it difficult even to say my prayers. There is hardly any amusement I would not rather take up than set myself to think of Thee. Give me grace, O my Father, to be utterly ashamed of my own reluctance! Rouse me from sloth and coldness, and make me desire Thee with my whole heart. Teach me to love meditation, sacred reading, and prayer. Teach me to love that which must engage my mind for all eternity.

Jesus Christ Yesterday and Today, and the Same Forever

1. All things change here below. I say it, O Lord; I believe it; and I shall feel it more and more the longer I live. Before Thy eyes, most awful Lord, the whole future of my life lies bare. Thou knowest exactly what will befall me every year and every day till my last hour. And, though I know not what Thou seest concerning me, so much I know, that is, that Thou dost read in my life perpetual change. Not a year will leave me as it found me, either within or without. I never shall remain any time in one state. How many things are sure to happen to me, unexpected, sudden, hard to bear! I know them not. I know not how long I have to live. I am hurried on, whether I will it or no, through continual change. O my God, what can I trust in? There is nothing I dare trust in; nay, did I trust in anything of earth, I believe for that very reason it would be taken away from me. I know Thou wouldest take it away, if Thou hadst love for me.

2. Everything short of Thee, O Lord, is changeable, but Thou endurest. Thou art ever one and the same. Ever the true God of man, and unchangeably so. Thou art the rarest, most precious, the sole good; and withal Thou art the most lasting. The creature changes, the Creator never. Then only the creature stops changing, when it rests on Thee. On Thee the Angels look and are at peace; that is why they have perfect bliss. They never can lose their blessedness, for they never can lose Thee. They have no anxiety, no misgivings—because they love the Creator; not any being of time and sense, but "Jesus Christ, the same yesterday and today, who is also forever."

3. My Lord, my Only God, "*Deus meus et omnia*," let me never go after vanities. "*Vanitas vanitatum et omnia vanitas.*" All is vanity and shadow here below. Let me not give my heart to anything here. Let nothing allure me from Thee; O keep me wholly and entirely. Keep thou this most frail heart and this most weak head in Thy Divine keeping. Draw me to Thee morning, noon, and night for consolation. Be Thou my own bright Light, to which I look, for guidance and for peace. Let me love Thee, O my Lord Jesus, with a pure affection and a fervent affection! Let me love Thee with the fervor, only greater, with which men of this earth love beings of this earth. Let me have that tenderness and constancy in loving Thee, which is so much praised among men, when the object is of the earth. Let me find and feel Thee to be my only joy, my only refuge, my only strength, my only comfort, my only hope, my only fear, my only love.

An Act of Love

1. My Lord, I believe, and know, and feel, that Thou art the Supreme Good. And, in saying so, I mean, not only supreme Goodness and Benevolence, but that Thou art the sovereign and transcendent Beautifulness. I believe that, beautiful as is Thy creation, it is mere dust and ashes, and of no account, compared with Thee, who art the infinitely more beautiful Creator. I know well, that therefore it is that the Angels and Saints have such perfect bliss, because they see Thee. To see even the glimpse of Thy true glory, even in this world throws holy men into an ecstasy. And I feel the truth of all this, in my own degree, because Thou hast mercifully taken our nature upon Thee, and hast come to me as man. *Et vidimus gloriam ejus, gloriam quasi Unigeniti a Patre*—"and we saw His glory, the glory as it were of the only begotten of the Father" (John 1:14). The more, O my dear Lord, I meditate on Thy words, works, actions, and sufferings in the Gospel, the more wonderfully glorious and beautiful I see Thee to be.

2. And therefore, O my dear Lord, since I perceive Thee to be so beautiful, I love Thee, and desire to love Thee more and more. Since Thou art the One Goodness, Beautifulness, Gloriousness, in the whole world of being, and there is nothing like Thee, but Thou art infinitely more glorious and good than even the most beautiful of creatures, therefore I love Thee with a singular love, a one, only, sovereign love. Everything, O my Lord, shall be dull and dim to me, after looking at Thee. There is nothing on earth, not even what is most naturally dear to me, that I can love in comparison of Thee. And I would lose everything whatever rather than lose Thee. For Thou, O my Lord, art my supreme and only Lord and love.

3. My God, Thou knowest infinitely better than I, how little I love Thee. I should not love Thee at all, except for Thy grace. It is Thy grace which has opened the eyes of my mind, and enabled them to see Thy glory. It is Thy grace which has touched my heart, and brought upon it the influence of what is so wonderfully beautiful and fair. How can I help loving Thee, O my Lord, except by some dreadful perversion, which hinders me from looking at Thee? O my God, whatever is nearer to me than Thou, things of this earth, and things more naturally pleasing to me, will be sure to interrupt the sight of Thee, unless Thy grace interfere. Keep Thou my eyes, my ears, my heart, from any such miserable tyranny. Break my bonds—raise my heart. Keep my whole being fixed on Thee. Let me never lose sight of Thee; and, while I gaze on Thee, let my love of Thee grow more and more every day.

IV

SIN

Against Thee Only Have I Sinned

1 Thou, O Lord, after living a whole eternity in ineffable bliss, because Thou art the one and sole Perfection, at length didst begin to create spirits to be with Thee and to share Thy blessedness according to their degree; and the return they made Thee was at once to rebel against Thee. First a great part of the Angels, then mankind, have risen up against Thee, and served others, not Thee. Why didst Thou create us, but to make us happy? Couldest Thou be made more happy by creating us? and how could we be happy but in obeying Thee? Yet we determined not to be happy as Thou wouldest have us happy, but to find out a happiness of our own; and so we left Thee. O my God, what a return is it that we—that I—make Thee when we sin! what dreadful unthankfulness is it!

and what will be my punishment for refusing to be happy, and for preferring hell to heaven! I know what the punishment will be; Thou wilt say, "Let him have it all his own way. He wishes to perish; let him perish. He despises the graces I give him; they shall turn to a curse."

2.   Thou, O my God, hast a claim on me, and I am wholly Thine! Thou art the Almighty Creator, and I am Thy workmanship. I am the work of Thy Hands, and Thou art my owner. As well might the axe or the hammer exalt itself against its framer, as I against Thee. Thou owest me nothing; I have no rights in respect to Thee, I have only duties. I depend on Thee for life, and health, and every blessing every moment. I have no more power of exercising will as to my life than axe or hammer. I depend on Thee far more entirely than anything here depends on its owner and master. The son does not depend on the father for the continuance of life—the matter out of which the axe is made existed first—but I depend wholly on Thee—if Thou withdraw Thy breath from me for a moment, I die. I am wholly and entirely Thy property and Thy work, and my one duty is to serve Thee.

3.   O my God, I confess that before now I have utterly forgotten this, and that I am continually forgetting it! I have acted many a time as if I were my own master, and turned from Thee rebelliously. I have acted according to my own pleasure, not according to Thine. And so far have I hardened myself, as not to feel as I ought how evil this is. I do not understand how dreadful sin is—and I do not hate it, and fear it, as I ought. I have no horror of it, or loathing. I do not turn from it with indignation, as being an insult to Thee, but I trifle with it, and, even if I do not commit great sins, I have no great reluctance to do small ones. O my God, what a great and awful difference is there between what I am and what I ought to be!

4. My God, I dare not offend any earthly superior; I am afraid—for I know I shall get into trouble—yet I dare offend Thee. I know, O Lord, that, according to the greatness of the person offended against, the greater is the offence. Yet I do not fear to offend Thee, whom to offend is to offend the infinite God. O my dear Lord, how should I myself feel, what should I say of myself, if I were to strike some revered superior on earth? if I were violently to deal a blow upon some one as revered as a father, or a priest; if I were to strike them on the face? I cannot bear even to think of such a thing—yet what is this compared with lifting up my hand against Thee? and what is sin but this? To sin is to insult Thee in the grossest of all conceivable ways. This then, O my soul! is what the sinfulness of sin consists in. It is lifting up my hand against my Infinite Benefactor, against my Almighty Creator, Preserver and Judge—against Him in whom all majesty and glory and beauty and reverence and sanctity center; against the one only God.

5. O my God, I am utterly confounded to think of the state in which I lie! What will become of me if Thou art severe? What is my life, O my dear and merciful Lord, but a series of offences, little or great, against Thee! O what great sins I have committed against Thee before now—and how continually in lesser matters I am sinning! My God, what will become of me? What will be my position hereafter if I am left to myself! What can I do but come humbly to Him whom I have so heavily affronted and insulted, and beg Him to forgive the debt which lies against me? O my Lord Jesus, whose love for me has been so great as to bring Thee down from heaven to save me, teach me, dear Lord, my sin—teach me its heinousness—teach me truly to repent of it—and pardon it in Thy great mercy!

6. I beg Thee, O my dear Savior, to recover me! Thy grace alone can do it. I cannot save myself. I cannot recover my lost ground. I cannot turn to Thee, I cannot please Thee, or save my soul without Thee. I shall go from bad to worse, I shall fall from Thee entirely, I shall quite harden myself against my neglect of duty, if I rely on my own strength. I shall make myself my center instead of making Thee. I shall worship some idol of my own framing instead of Thee, the only true God and my Maker, unless Thou hinder it by Thy grace. O my dear Lord, hear me! I have lived long enough in this undecided, wavering, unsatisfactory state. I wish to be Thy good servant. I wish to sin no more. Be gracious to me, and enable me to be what I know I ought to be.

The Effects of Sin

1. My Lord, Thou art the infinitely merciful God. Thou lovest all things that Thou hast created. Thou art the lover of souls. How then is it, O Lord, that I am in a world so miserable as this is? Can this be the world which Thou hast created, so full of pain and suffering? Who among the sons of Adam lives without suffering from his birth to his death? How many bad sicknesses and diseases are there! how many frightful accidents! how many great anxieties! how are men brought down and broken by grief, distress, the tumult of passions, and continual fear! What dreadful plagues are there ever on the earth: war, famine, and pestilence! Why is this, O my God? Why is this, O my soul? Dwell upon it, and ask thyself, Why is this? Has God changed His nature? yet how evil has the earth become!

2. O my God, I know full well why all these evils are. Thou hast not changed Thy nature, but man has ruined his own. We have sinned, O Lord, and therefore is this change. All these evils which I see and in which I partake are the fruit of sin. They would not

have been, had we not sinned. They are but the first instalment of the punishment of sin. They are an imperfect and dim image of what sin is. Sin is infinitely worse than famine, than war, than pestilence. Take the most hideous of diseases, under which the body wastes away and corrupts, the blood is infected; the head, the heart, the lungs, every organ disordered, the nerves unstrung and shattered; pain in every limb, thirst, restlessness, delirium—all is nothing compared with that dreadful sickness of the soul which we call sin. They all are the effects of it, they all are shadows of it, but nothing more. That cause itself is something different in kind, is of a malignity far other and greater than all these things. O my God, teach me this! Give me to understand the enormity of that evil under which I labor and know it not. Teach me what sin is.

3. All these dreadful pains of body and soul are the fruits of sin, but they are nothing to its punishment in the world to come. The keenest and fiercest of bodily pains is nothing to the fire of hell; the most dire horror or anxiety is nothing to the never-dying worm of conscience; the greatest bereavement, loss of substance, desertion of friends, and forlorn desolation is nothing compared to the loss of God's countenance. Eternal punishment is the only true measure of the guilt of sin. My God, teach me this. Open my eyes and heart, I earnestly pray Thee, and make me understand how awful a body of death I bear about me. And, not only teach me about it, but in Thy mercy and by Thy grace remove it.

The Evil of Sin

1. My God, I know that Thou didst create the whole universe very good; and if this was true of the material world which we see, much more true is it of the world of rational beings. The innumerable

stars which fill the firmament, and the very elements out of which the earth is made, all are carried through their courses and their operations in perfect concord; but much higher was the concord which reigned in heaven when the Angels were first created. At that first moment of their existence the main orders of the Angels were in the most excellent harmony, and beautiful to contemplate; and the creation of man was expected next, to continue that harmony in the instance of a different kind of being. Then it was that suddenly was discovered a flaw or a rent in one point of this most delicate and exquisite web—and it extended and unraveled the web, till a third part of it was spoilt; and then again, a similar flaw was found in human kind, and it extended over the whole race. This dreadful evil, destroying so large a portion of all God's works, is sin.

2. My God, such is sin in Thy judgment; what is it in the judgment of the world? A very small evil or none at all. In the judgment of the Creator it is that which has marred His spiritual work; it is a greater evil than though the stars got loose, and ran wild in heaven, and chaos came again. But man, who is the guilty one, calls it by soft names. He explains it away. The world laughs at it, and is indulgent to it; and, as to its deserving eternal punishment, it rises up indignant at the idea, and rather than admit it, would deny the God who has said it does. The world thinks sin the same sort of imperfection as an impropriety, or want of taste or infirmity. O my soul, consider carefully the great difference between the views of sin taken by Almighty God and the world! Which of the two views do you mean to believe?

3. O my soul, which of the two wilt thou believe—the word of God or the word of man? Is God right or is the creature right? Is sin the greatest of all possible evils or the least? My Lord and Savior, I have

no hesitation which to believe. Thou art true, and every man a liar. I will believe Thee, above the whole world. My God, imprint on my heart the infamous deformity of sin. Teach me to abhor it as a pestilence—as a fierce flame destroying on every side; as my death. Let me take up arms against it, and devote myself to fight under Thy banner in overcoming it.

The Heinousness of Sin

1. My Lord, I know well that Thou art all perfect, and needest nothing. Yet I know that Thou hast taken upon Thyself the nature of man, and, not only so, but in that nature didst come upon earth, and suffer all manner of evil, and didst die. This is a history which has hung the heavens with sackcloth, and taken from this earth, beautiful as it is, its light and glory. Thou didst come, O my dear Lord, and Thou didst suffer in no ordinary way, but unheard of and extreme torments! The all-blessed Lord suffered the worst and most various of pains. This is the corner truth of the Gospel: it is the one foundation, Jesus Christ and He crucified. I know it, O Lord, I believe it, and I put it steadily before me.

2. Why is this strange anomaly in the face of nature? Does God do things for naught? No, my soul, it is sin; it is thy sin, which has brought the Everlasting down upon earth to suffer. Hence, I learn how great an evil sin is. The death of the Infinite is its sole measure. All that slow distress of body and mind which He endured, from the time He shed blood at Gethsemani down to His death, all that pain came from sin. What sort of evil is that, which had to be so encountered by such a sacrifice, and to be reversed at such a price! Here then I understand best how horrible a thing sin is. It is horrible; because through it have come upon men all those

evils whatever they are, with which the earth abounds. It is more horrible, in that it has nailed the Son of God to the accursed tree.

3. My dear Lord and Savior, how can I make light of that which has had such consequences! Henceforth I will, through Thy grace, have deeper views of sin than before. Fools make jest of sin, but I will view things in their true light. My suffering Lord, I have made Thee suffer. Thou art most beautiful in Thy eternal nature, O my Lord; Thou art most beautiful in Thy sufferings! Thy adorable attributes are not dimmed, but increased to us as we gaze on Thy humiliation. Thou art more beautiful to us than before. But still I will never forget that it was man's sin, my sin, which made that humiliation necessary. *Amor meus crucifixus est*—"my Love is crucified," but by none other than me. I have crucified Thee; my sin has crucified Thee. O my Savior, what a dreadful thought—but I cannot undo it; all I can do is to hate that which made Thee suffer. Shall I not do that at least? Shall I not love my Lord just so much as to hate that which is so great an enemy of His, and break off all terms with it? Shall I not put off sin altogether? By Thy great love of me, teach me and enable me to do this, O Lord. Give me a deep, rooted, intense hatred of sin.

The Bondage of Sin

1. Thou, O my Lord and God, Thou alone art strong, Thou alone holy! Thou art the *Sanctus Deus, Sanctus fortis*—"Holy God, holy and strong!" Thou art the sanctity and the strength of all things. No created nature has any stay or subsistence in itself, but crumbles and melts away, if Thou art not with it, to sustain it. My God, Thou art the strength of the Angels, of the Saints in glory—of holy men on earth. No being has any sanctity or any strength apart from Thee.

My God, I wish to adore Thee as such. I wish with all my heart to understand and to confess this great truth, that not only Thou art Almighty, but that there is no might at all, or power, or strength, anywhere but in Thee.

2. My God, if Thou art the strength of all spirits, O how pre-eminently art Thou my strength! O how true it is, so that nothing is more so, that I have no strength but in Thee! I feel intimately, O my God, that, whenever I am left to myself, I go wrong. As sure as a stone falls down to the earth if it be let go, so surely my heart and spirit fall down hopelessly if they are let go by Thee. Thou must uphold me by Thy right hand, or I cannot stand. How strange it is, but how true, that all my natural tendencies are towards sloth, towards excess, towards neglect of religion, towards neglect of prayer, towards love of the world, not towards love of Thee, or love of sanctity, or love of self-governance. I approve and praise what I do not do. My heart runs after vanities, and I tend to death, I tend to corruption and dissolution, apart from Thee, *Deus immortalis*.

3. My God, I have had experience enough what a dreadful bondage sin is. If Thou art away, I find I cannot keep myself, however I wish it—and am in the hands of my own self-will, pride, sensuality, and selfishness. And they prevail with me more and more every day, till they are irresistible. In time the old Adam within me gets so strong, that I become a mere slave. I confess things to be wrong which nevertheless I do. I bitterly lament over my bondage, but I cannot undo it. O what a tyranny is sin! It is a heavy weight which cripples me—and what will be the end of it? By Thy all-precious merits, by Thy Almighty power, I entreat Thee, O my Lord, to give me life and sanctity and strength! *Deus sanctus*, give me holiness; *Deus fortis*, give me strength; *Deus immortalis*, give me perseverance. *Sanctus Deus, Sanctus fortis, Sanctus immortalis, miserere nobis.*

Every Sin Has its Punishment

1 Thou art the all-seeing, all-knowing God. Thy eyes, O Lord, are in every place. Thou art a real spectator of everything which takes place anywhere. Thou art ever with me. Thou art present and conscious of all I think, say, or do. *Tu Deus qui vidisti me—* "Thou, God, who hast seen me." Every deed or act, however slight; every word, however quick and casual; every thought of my heart, however secret, however momentary, however forgotten, Thou seest, O Lord, Thou seest and Thou notest down. Thou hast a book; Thou enterest in it every day of my life. I forget; Thou dost not forget. There is stored up the history of all my past years, and so it will be till I die—the leaves will be filled and turned over—and the book at length finished. *Quo ibo a Spiritu Tuo—*"whither shall I go from Thy Spirit?" (Psalm 139:7). I am in Thy hands, O Lord, absolutely.

2. My God, how often do I act wrongly, how seldom rightly! how dreary on the whole are the acts of any one day! All my sins, offences, and negligences, not of one day only, but of all days, are in Thy book. And every sin, offence, negligence, has a separate definite punishment. That list of penalties increases, silently but surely, every day. As the spendthrift is overwhelmed by a continually greater weight of debt, so am I exposed continually to a greater and greater score of punishments catalogued against me. I forget the sins of my childhood, my boyhood, my adolescence, my youth. They are all noted down in that book. There is a complete history of all my life; and it will one day be brought up against me. Nothing is lost, all is remembered. O my soul, what hast thou to go through! What an examination that will be, and what a result! I shall have put upon me the punishment of ten thousand sins—I shall for this purpose be sent to Purgatory—how long will it last?

when shall I ever get out? Not till I have paid the last farthing.
When will this possibly be?

3. O my dear Lord, have mercy upon me! I trust Thou hast forgiven
    me my sins—but the punishment remains. In the midst of Thy
    love for me, and recognizing me as Thine own, Thou wilt consign
    me to Purgatory. There I shall go through my sins once more, in
    their punishment. There I shall suffer, but here is the time for a
    thorough repentance. Here is the time of good works, of obtaining
    indulgences, of wiping out the debt in every possible way. Thy saints,
    though to the eyes of man without sin, really had a vast account—
    and they settled it by continual trials here. I have neither their merit
    nor their sufferings. I cannot tell whether I can make such acts of
    love as will gain me an indulgence of my sins. The prospect before
    me is dark—I can only rely on Thy infinite compassion. O my dear
    Lord, who hast in so many ways shown Thy mercy towards me, pity
    me here! Be merciful in the midst of justice.

V

The Power of the Cross

1. My God, who could have imagined, by any light of nature, that
    it was one of Thy attributes to lower Thyself, and to work out
    Thy purposes by Thy own humiliation and suffering? Thou hadst
    lived from eternity in ineffable blessedness. My God, I might
    have understood as much as this, namely that, when Thou didst
    begin to create and surround Thyself with a world of creatures,
    that these attributes would show themselves in Thee which before
    had no exercise. Thou couldest not show Thy power when there
    was nothing whatever to exercise it. Then too, Thou didst begin
    to show thy wonderful and tender providence, Thy faithfulness,

Thy solicitous care for those whom Thou hadst created. But who could have fancied that Thy creation of the universe implied and involved in it Thy humiliation? O my great God, Thou hast humbled Thyself, Thou hast stooped to take our flesh and blood, and hast been lifted up upon the tree! I praise and glorify Thee tenfold the more, because Thou hast shown Thy power by means of Thy suffering, than hadst Thou carried on Thy work without it. It is worthy of Thy infinitude thus to surpass and transcend all our thoughts.

2. O my Lord Jesu, I believe, and by Thy grace will ever believe and hold, and I know that it is true, and will be true to the end of the world, that nothing great is done without suffering, without humiliation, and that all things are possible by means of it. I believe, O my God, that poverty is better than riches, pain better than pleasure, obscurity and contempt than name, and ignominy and reproach than honor. My Lord, I do not ask Thee to bring these trials on me, for I know not if I could face them; but at least, O Lord, whether I be in prosperity or adversity, I will believe that it is as I have said. I will never have faith in riches, rank, power, or reputation. I will never set my heart on worldly success or on worldly advantages. I will never wish for what men call the prizes of life. I will ever, with Thy grace, make much of those who are despised or neglected, honor the poor, revere the suffering, and admire and venerate Thy saints and confessors, and take my part with them in spite of the world.

3. And lastly, O my dear Lord, though I am so very weak that I am not fit to ask Thee for suffering as a gift, and have not strength to do so, at least I will beg of Thee grace to meet suffering well, when Thou in Thy love and wisdom dost bring it upon me. Let me bear pain, reproach, disappointment, slander, anxiety, suspense, as

Thou wouldest have me, O my Jesu, and as Thou by Thy own suffering hast taught me, when it comes. And I promise too, with Thy grace, that I will never set myself up, never seek pre-eminence, never court any great thing of the world, never prefer myself to others. I wish to bear insult meekly, and to return good for evil. I wish to humble myself in all things, and to be silent when I am ill-used, and to be patient when sorrow or pain is prolonged, and all for the love of Thee, and Thy Cross, knowing that in this way I shall gain the promise both of this life and of the next.

VI

The Resurrection

The Temples of the Holy Ghost

1. I adore Thee, O Eternal Word, for Thy gracious condescension, in not only taking a created nature, a created spirit or soul, but a material body. The Most High decreed that for ever and ever He would subject Himself to a created prison. He who from eternity was nothing but infinite incomprehensible Spirit, beyond all laws but those of His own transcendent Greatness, willed that for the eternity to come He should be united, in the most intimate of unions, with that which was under the conditions of a creature. Thy omnipotence, O Lord, ever protects itself—but nothing short of that omnipotence could enable Thee so to condescend without a loss of power. Thy Body has part in Thy power, rather than Thou hast part in its weakness. For this reason, my God, it was, that Thou couldst not but rise again, if Thou wast to die—because Thy Body, once taken by Thee, never was or could be separated from Thee, even in the grave. It was Thy Body even then, it could see no corruption; it could not remain under the power of death, for

Thou hadst already wonderfully made it Thine, and whatever was Thine must last in its perfection forever. I adore Thy Most Holy Body, O my dear Jesus, the instrument of our redemption!

2. I look at Thee, my Lord Jesus, and think of Thy Most Holy Body, and I keep it before me as the pledge of my own resurrection. Though I die, as die I certainly shall, nevertheless I shall not for ever die, for I shall rise again. My Lord, the heathen who knew Thee not, thought the body to be of a miserable and contemptible nature—they thought it the seat, the cause, the excuse of all moral evil. When their thoughts soared highest, and they thought of a future life, they considered that the destruction of the body was the condition of that higher existence. That the body was really part of themselves and that its restoration could be a privilege, was beyond their utmost imagination. And indeed, what mind of man, O Lord, could ever have fancied without Thy revelation that what, according to our experience, is so vile, so degraded, so animal, so sinful, which is our fellowship with the brutes, which is full of corruption and becomes dust and ashes, was in its very nature capable of so high a destiny! that it could become celestial and immortal, without ceasing to be a body! And who but Thou, who art omnipotent, could have made it so! No wonder then, that the wise men of the world, who did not believe in Thee, scoffed at the Resurrection. But I, by Thy grace, will ever keep before me how differently I have been taught by Thee. O best and first and truest of Teachers! O Thou who art the Truth, I know, and believe with my whole heart, that this very flesh of mine will rise again. I know, base and odious as it is at present, that it will one day, if I be worthy, be raised incorruptible and altogether beautiful and glorious. This I know; this, by Thy grace, I will ever keep before me.

3. O my God, teach me so to live, as one who does believe the great
    dignity, the great sanctity of that material frame in which Thou hast
    lodged me. And therefore, O my dear Saviour! do I come so often
    and so earnestly to be partaker of Thy Body and Blood, that by
    means of Thy own ineffable holiness I may be made holy. O my
    Lord Jesus, I know what is written, that our bodies are the temples
    of the Holy Ghost. Should I not venerate that which Thou dost
    miraculously feed, and which Thy Co-equal Spirit inhabits! O my
    God, who wast nailed to the Cross, *confige timore tuo carnes meas*—
    "pierce Thou my flesh with Thy fear" (Psalm 119:120); crucify my
    soul and body in all that is sinful in them, and make me pure as
    Thou art pure.

God Alone

Thomas says to Him, "My Lord and my God." (JOHN 20:28)

1. I adore Thee, O my God, with Thomas; and if I have, like him,
    sinned through unbelief, I adore Thee the more. I adore Thee as the
    One Adorable, I adore Thee as more glorious in Thy humiliation,
    when men despised Thee, than when Angels worshipped Thee.
    Deus meus et omnia—"My God and my all." To have Thee is to
    have everything I can have. O my Eternal Father, give me Thyself.
    I dared not have made so bold a request, it would have been
    presumption, unless Thou hadst encouraged me. Thou hast put
    it into my mouth, Thou hast clothed Thyself in my nature, Thou
    hast become my Brother, Thou hast died as other men die, only
    in far greater bitterness, that, instead of my eyeing Thee fearfully
    from afar, I might confidently draw near to Thee. Thou dost speak
    to me as Thou didst speak to Thomas, and dost beckon me to take
    hold of Thee. My God and my all, what could I say more than

this, if I spoke to all eternity! I am full and abound and overflow, when I have Thee; but without Thee I am nothing—I wither away, I dissolve and perish. My Lord and my God, my God and my all, give me Thyself and nothing else.

2   Thomas came and touched Thy sacred wounds. O will the day ever come when I shall be allowed actually and visibly to kiss them? What a day will that be when I am thoroughly cleansed from all impurity and sin, and am fit to draw near to my Incarnate God in His palace of light above! What a morning, when having done with all penal suffering, I see Thee for the first time with these very eyes of mine, I see Thy countenance, gaze upon Thy eyes and gracious lips without quailing, and then kneel down with joy to kiss Thy feet, and am welcomed into Thy arms. O my only true Lover, the only Lover of my soul, Thee will I love now, that I may love Thee then. What a day, a long day without ending, the day of eternity, when I shall be so unlike what I am now, when I feel in myself a body of death, and am perplexed and distracted with ten thousand thoughts, any one of which would keep me from heaven. O my Lord, what a day when I shall have done once for all with all sins, venial as well as mortal, and shall stand perfect and acceptable in Thy sight, able to bear Thy presence, nothing shrinking from Thy eye, not shrinking from the pure scrutiny of Angels and Archangels, when I stand in the midst and they around me!

3.   O my God, though I am not fit to see or touch Thee yet, still I will ever come within Thy reach, and desire that which is not yet given me in its fullness. O my Savior, Thou shalt be my sole God!—I will have no Lord but Thee. I will break to pieces all idols in my heart which rival Thee. I will have nothing but Jesus and Him crucified. It shall be my life to pray to Thee, to offer myself to Thee, to keep

Thee before me, to worship Thee in Thy holy Sacrifice, and to surrender myself to Thee in Holy Communion.

The Forbearance of Jesus

"See my hands," etc. "Have you anything here to eat?"
(JOHN 20:27, LUKE 24:41)

1. I adore Thee, O my Lord, for Thy wonderful patience and Thy compassionate tenderhearted condescension. Thy disciples, in spite of all Thy teaching and miracles, disbelieved Thee when they saw Thee die, and fled. Nor did they take courage afterwards, nor think of Thy promise of rising again on the third day. They did not believe Magdalen, nor the other women, who said they had seen Thee alive again. Yet Thou didst appear to them—Thou didst show them Thy wounds—Thou didst let them touch Thee—Thou didst eat before them, and give them Thy peace. O Jesu, is any obstinacy too great for Thy love? does any number of falls and relapses vanquish the faithfulness and endurance of Thy compassion? Thou dost forgive not only seven times, but to seventy times seven. Many waters cannot quench a love like Thine. And such Thou art all over the earth, even to the end—forgiving, sparing, forbearing, waiting, though sinners are ever provoking Thee; pitying and taking into account their ignorance, visiting all men, all Thine enemies, with the gentle pleadings of Thy grace, day after day, year after year, up to the hour of their death—for He knoweth whereof we are made; He knoweth we are but dust.

2. My God, what hast Thou done for me! Men say of Thee, O my only Good, that Thy judgments are severe, and Thy punishments excessive. All I can say is, that I have not found them so in my

own case. Let others speak for themselves, and Thou wilt meet and overcome them to their own confusion in the day of reckoning. With them I have nothing to do—Thou wilt settle with them—but for me the only experience that I have is Thy dealings with myself, and here I bear witness, as I know so entirely and feel so intimately, that to me Thou hast been nothing but forbearance and mercy. O how Thou dost forget that I have ever rebelled against Thee! Again and again dost Thou help me. I fall, yet Thou dost not cast me off. In spite of all my sins, Thou dost still love me, prosper me, comfort me, surround me with blessings, sustain me, and further me. I grieve Thy good grace, yet Thou dost give more. I insult Thee, yet Thou never dost take offence, but art as kind as if I had nothing to explain, to repent of, to amend—as if I were Thy best, most faithful, most steady and loyal friend. Nay, alas! I am even led to presume upon Thy love, it is so like easiness and indulgence, though I ought to fear Thee. I confess it, O my true Savior, every day is but a fresh memorial of Thy unwearied, unconquerable love!

3. O my God, suffer me still—bear with me in spite of my waywardness, perverseness, and ingratitude! I improve very slowly, but really I am moving on to heaven, or at least I wish to move. I am putting Thee before me, vile sinner as I am, and I am really thinking in earnest of saving my soul. Give me time to collect my thoughts, and make one good effort. I protest I will put off this languor and lukewarmness—I will shake myself from this sullenness and despondency and gloom—I will rouse myself, and be cheerful, and walk in Thy light. I will have no hope or joy but Thee. Only give me Thy grace—meet me with Thy grace, I will through Thy grace do what I can—and Thou shalt perfect it for me. Then I shall have happy days in Thy presence, and in the sight and adoration of Thy five Sacred Wounds.

VII
GOD WITH US

The Familiarity of Jesus

1. The Holy Baptist was separated from the world. He was a
    Nazarite. He went out from the world, and placed himself over
    against it, and spoke to it from his vantage ground, and called it
    to repentance. Then went out all Jerusalem to him into the desert,
    and he confronted it face to face. But in his teaching, he spoke of
    One who should come to them and speak to them in a far different
    way. He should not separate Himself from them, He should not
    display Himself as some higher being, but as their brother, as of
    their flesh and of their bones, as one among many brethren, as
    one of the multitude and amidst them; nay, He was among them
    already. "*Medius vestrum stetit, quem vos nescitis*"—"there hath
    stood in the midst of you, whom you know not." That greater
    one called Himself the Son of man—He was content to be taken
    as ordinary in all respects, though He was the Highest. St. John
    and the other Evangelists, though so different in the character of
    their accounts of Him, agree most strikingly here. The Baptist says,
    "There is in the midst of you One whom you know not" (John
    1:26). Next, we read of his pointing Jesus out privately, not to
    crowds, but to one or two of his own religious followers; then of
    their seeking Jesus and being allowed to follow Him home. At
    length Jesus begins to disclose Himself and to manifest His glory
    in miracles; but where? At a marriage feast, where there was often
    excess, as the architriclinus[4] implies. And how? in adding to the
    wine, the instrument of such excess, when it occurred. He was at
    that marriage feast not as a teacher, but as a guest, and (so to speak)
    in a social way, for He was with His Mother. Now compare this

---

4 An uncommon word meaning master of the feast, the one who presides at table.

with what He says in St. Matthew's Gospel of Himself: "John came neither eating nor drinking—The Son of man came eating and drinking, and they say: Behold a man that is a glutton and wine-drinker." John might be hated, but he was respected; Jesus was despised. See also Mark 1:22, 27, 37; 3:21, for the astonishment and rudeness of all about Him. The objection occurs at once, 2:16. What a marked feature it must have been of our Lord's character and mission, since two Evangelists, so independent in their narrations, record it! The prophet had said the same (Isaiah 53 "He shall," etc.).

2. This was, O dear Lord, because Thou so lovest this human nature which Thou hast created. Thou didst not love us merely as Thy creatures, the work of Thy hands, but as men. Thou lovest all, for Thou hast created all; but Thou lovest man more than all. How is it, Lord, that this should be? What is there in man, above others? *Quid est homo, quod memor es ejus?* yet, *nusquam Angelos apprehendit*—"What is man, that Thou art mindful of him?" . . . "nowhere doth he take hold of the angels." Who can sound the depth of Thy counsels and decrees? Thou hast loved man more than Thou hast loved the Angels: and therefore, as Thou didst not take on Thee an angelic nature when Thou didst manifest Thyself for our salvation, so too Thou wouldest not come in any shape or capacity or office which was above the course of ordinary human life—not as a Nazarene, not as a Levitical priest, not as a monk, not as a hermit, but in the fulness and exactness of that human nature which so much Thou lovest. Thou camest not only a perfect man, but as proper man; not formed anew out of earth, not with the spiritual body which Thou now hast, but in that very flesh which had fallen in Adam, and with all our infirmities, all our feelings and sympathies, sin excepted.

3. O Jesu, it became Thee, the great God, thus abundantly and largely to do Thy work, for which the Father sent Thee. Thou didst not do it by halves—and, while that magnificence of Sacrifice is Thy glory as God, it is our consolation and aid as sinners. O dearest Lord, Thou art more fully man than the holy Baptist, than St. John, Apostle and Evangelist, than Thy own sweet Mother. As in Divine knowledge of me Thou art beyond them all, so also in experience and personal knowledge of my nature. Thou art my elder brother. How can I fear, how should I not repose my whole heart on one so gentle, so tender, so familiar, so unpretending, so modest, so natural, so humble? Thou art now, though in heaven, just the same as Thou wast on earth: the mighty God, yet the little child—the all-holy, yet the all-sensitive, all-human.

Jesus the Hidden God

"Be not faithless, but believing." (JOHN 20:27)

1. I adore Thee, O my God, who art so awful, because Thou art hidden and unseen! I adore Thee, and I desire to live by faith in what I do not see; and considering what I am, a disinherited outcast, I think it has indeed gone well with me that I am allowed, O my unseen Lord and Savior, to worship Thee anyhow. O my God, I know that it is sin that has separated between Thee and me. I know it is sin that has brought on me the penalty of ignorance. Adam, before he fell, was visited by Angels. Thy Saints, too, who keep close to Thee, see visions, and in many ways are brought into sensible perception of Thy presence. But to a sinner such as I am, what is left but to possess Thee without seeing Thee? Ah, should I not rejoice at having that most extreme mercy and favor of possessing Thee at all? It is sin that has reduced me to live by faith, as I must at best,

and should I not rejoice in such a life, O Lord my God? I see and know, O my good Jesus, that the only way in which I can possibly approach Thee in this world is the way of faith, faith in what Thou hast told me, and I thankfully follow this only way which Thou hast given me.

2.   O my God, Thou dost over-abound in mercy! To live by faith is my necessity, from my present state of being and from my sin; but Thou hast pronounced a blessing on it. Thou hast said that I am more blessed if I believe on Thee, than if I saw Thee. Give me to share that blessedness, give it to me in its fullness. Enable me to believe as if I saw; let me have Thee always before me as if Thou wert always bodily and sensibly present. Let me ever hold communion with Thee, my hidden, but my living God. Thou art in my innermost heart. Thou art the life of my life. Every breath I breathe, every thought of my mind, every good desire of my heart, is from the presence within me of the unseen God. By nature and by grace Thou art in me. I see Thee not in the material world except dimly, but I recognize Thy voice in my own intimate consciousness. I turn round and say *Rabboni*. O be ever thus with me; and if I am tempted to leave Thee, do not Thou, O my God, leave me!

3.   O my dear Savior, would that I had any right to ask to be allowed to make reparation to Thee for all the unbelief of the world, and all the insults offered to Thy Name, Thy Word, Thy Church, and the Sacrament of Thy Love! But, alas, I have a long score of unbelief and ingratitude of my own to atone for. Thou art in the Sacrifice of the Mass, Thou art in the Tabernacle, verily and indeed, in flesh and blood; and the world not only disbelieves, but mocks at this gracious truth. Thou didst warn us long ago by Thyself and by Thy Apostles that Thou wouldest hide Thyself from the world.

The prophecy is fulfilled more than ever now; but I know what the world knows not. O accept my homage, my praise, my adoration!—let me at least not be found wanting. I cannot help the sins of others—but one at least of those whom Thou hast redeemed shall turn round and with a loud voice glorify God. The more men scoff, the more will I believe in Thee, the good God, the good Jesus, the hidden Lord of life, who hast done me nothing else but good from the very first moment that I began to live.

Jesus the Light of the Soul

"Stay with us, because it is towards evening." (LUKE 24:29)

1. I adore Thee, O my God, as the true and only Light! From Eternity to Eternity, before any creature was, when Thou wast alone, alone but not solitary, for Thou hast ever been Three in One, Thou wast the Infinite Light. There was none to see Thee but Thyself. The Father saw that Light in the Son, and the Son in the Father. Such as Thou wast in the beginning, such Thou art now. Most separate from all creatures in this Thy uncreated Brightness. Most glorious, most beautiful. Thy attributes are so many separate and resplendent colours, each as perfect in its own purity and grace as if it were the sole and highest perfection. Nothing created is more than the very shadow of Thee. Bright as are the Angels, they are poor and most unworthy shadows of Thee. They pale and look dim and gather blackness before Thee. They are so feeble beside Thee, that they are unable to gaze upon Thee. The highest Seraphim veil their eyes, by deed as well as by word proclaiming Thy unutterable glory. For me, I cannot even look upon the sun, and what is this but a base material emblem of Thee? How should I endure to look even on an

Angel? and how could I look upon Thee and live? If I were placed in the illumination of Thy countenance, I should shrink up like the grass. O most gracious God, who shall approach Thee, being so glorious, yet how can I keep from Thee?

2. How can I keep from Thee? For Thou, who art the Light of Angels, art the only Light of my soul. Thou enlightenest every man that cometh into this world. I am utterly dark, as dark as hell, without Thee. I droop and shrink when Thou art away. I revive only in proportion as Thou dawnest upon me. Thou comest and goest at Thy will. O my God, I cannot keep Thee! I can only beg of Thee to stay. "*Mane nobiscum, Domine, quoniam advesperascit.*" Remain till morning, and then go not without giving me a blessing. Remain with me till death in this dark valley, when the darkness will end. Remain, O Light of my soul, *jam advesperascit!* The gloom, which is not Thine, falls over me. I am nothing. I have little command of myself. I cannot do what I would. I am disconsolate and sad. I want something, I know not what. It is Thou that I want, though I so little understand this. I say it and take it on faith; I partially understand it, but very poorly. Shine on me, *O Ignis semper ardens et nunquam deficiens!*—"O fire ever burning and never failing" (Exodus 3:2)—and I shall begin, through and in Thy Light, to see Light, and to recognize Thee truly, as the Source of Light. *Mane nobiscum*; stay, sweet Jesus, stay forever. In this decay of nature, give more grace.

3. Stay with me, and then I shall begin to shine as Thou shinest: so to shine as to be a light to others. The light, O Jesus, will be all from Thee. None of it will be mine. No merit to me. It will be Thou who shinest through me upon others. O let me thus praise Thee, in the way which Thou dost love best, by shining on all those around me. Give light to them as well as to me; light them with

me, through me. Teach me to show forth Thy praise, Thy truth, Thy will. Make me preach Thee without preaching—not by words, but by my example and by the catching force, the sympathetic influence, of what I do—by my visible resemblance to Thy saints, and the evident fullness of the love which my heart bears to Thee.

VIII
GOD ALL-SUFFICIENT

"Show us the Father, and it is enough for us. . . .
Philip, he that seeth Me, seeth the Father also." (JOHN 14:8–9)

1. The Son is in the Father and the Father in the Son. O adorable mystery which has been from eternity! I adore Thee, O my incomprehensible Creator, before whom I am an atom, a being of yesterday or an hour ago! Go back a few years and I simply did not exist; I was not in being, and things went on without me: but Thou art from eternity; and nothing whatever for one moment could go on without Thee. And from eternity too Thou hast possessed Thy Nature; Thou hast been—this awful glorious mystery—the Son in the Father and the Father in the Son. Whether we be in existence, or whether we be not, Thou art one and the same always, the Son sufficient for the Father, the Father for the Son—and all other things, in themselves, but vanity. All things once were not, all things might not be, but it would be enough for the Father that He had begotten His co-equal consubstantial Son, and for the Son that He was embraced in the Bosom of the Eternal Father. O adorable mystery! Human reason has not conducted me to it, but I believe. I believe, because Thou hast spoken, O Lord. I joyfully accept Thy word about Thyself. Thou must know what Thou art—and who else? Not I surely, dust and ashes, except so far

as Thou tellest me. I take then Thy own witness, O my Creator! and I believe firmly, I repeat after Thee, what I do not understand, because I wish to live a life of faith; and I prefer faith in Thee to trust in myself.

2. O my great God, from eternity Thou wast sufficient for Thyself! The Father was sufficient for the Son, and the Son for the Father; art Thou not then sufficient for me, a poor creature, Thou so great, I so little! I have a double all-sufficiency in the Father and the Son. I will take then St. Philip's word and say, Show us the Father, and it suffices us. It suffices us, for then are we full to overflowing, when we have Thee. O mighty God, strengthen me with Thy strength, console me with Thy everlasting peace, soothe me with the beauty of Thy countenance; enlighten me with Thy uncreated brightness; purify me with the fragrance of Thy ineffable holiness. Bathe me in Thyself, and give me to drink, as far as mortal man may ask, of the rivers of grace which flow from the Father and the Son, the grace of Thy consubstantial, co-eternal Love.

3. O my God, let me never forget this truth—that not only art Thou my Life, but my only Life! Thou art the Way, the Truth, and the Life. Thou art my Life, and the Life of all who live. All men, all I know, all I meet, all I see and hear of, live not unless they live by Thee. They live in Thee, or else they live not at all. No one can be saved out of Thee. Let me never forget this in the business of the day. O give me a true love of souls, of those souls for whom Thou didst die. Teach me to pray for their conversion, to do my part towards effecting it. However able they are, however amiable, however high and distinguished, they cannot be saved unless they have Thee. O my all-sufficient Lord, Thou only sufficest! Thy blood is sufficient for the whole world. As Thou art sufficient for me, so Thou art sufficient for the entire race of Adam. O my Lord

Jesus, let Thy Cross be more than sufficient for them, let it be effectual! Let it be effectual for me more than all, lest I "have all and abound," yet bring no fruit to perfection.

IX
GOD ALONE UNCHANGEABLE

"Whither I go, thou canst not follow Me now, but thou shalt follow hereafter." (JOHN 13:36)

1. Thou alone, O my God, art what Thou ever hast been! Man changes. Thou art unchangeable; nay, even as man Thou hast ever been unchangeable, for Jesus is yesterday and today Himself, and forever. Thy word endureth in heaven and earth. Thy decrees are fixed; Thy gifts are without repentance. Thy Nature, Thy Attributes, are ever the same. There ever was Father, ever Son, ever Holy Ghost. I adore Thee in the peace and serenity of Thy unchangeableness. I adore Thee in that imperturbable heaven, which is Thyself. Thou wast perfect from the first; nothing couldest Thou gain, and nothing mightest Thou lose. There was nothing that could touch Thee, because there was nothing but what Thou didst create and couldst destroy. Again, I adore Thee in this Thy infinite stability, which is the center and stay of all created things.

2. Man on the contrary is ever changing. Not a day passes but I am nearer the grave. Whatever be my age, whatever the number of my years, I am ever narrowing the interval between time and eternity. I am ever changing in myself. Youth is not like age; and I am continually changing, as I pass along out of youth towards the end of life. O my God, I am crumbling away, as I go on! I am already dissolving into my first elements. My soul indeed cannot die, for

Thou hast made it immortal; but my bodily frame is continually resolving into that dust out of which it was taken. All below heaven changes: spring, summer, autumn, each has its turn. The fortunes of the world change; what was high, lies low; what was low rises high. Riches take wings and flee away; bereavements happen. Friends become enemies, and enemies, friends. Our wishes, aims, and plans change. There is nothing stable but Thou, O my God! And Thou art the center and life of all who change, who trust Thee as their Father, who look to Thee, and who are content to put themselves into Thy hands.

3. I know, O my God, I must change, if I am to see Thy face! I must undergo the change of death. Body and soul must die to this world. My real self, my soul, must change by a true regeneration. None but the holy can see Thee. Like Peter, I cannot have a blessing now, which I shall have afterwards. "Thou canst not follow me now, but thou shalt follow hereafter" (John 13:36). Oh, support me, as I proceed in this great, awful, happy change, with the grace of Thy unchangeableness. My unchangeableness here below is perseverance in changing. Let me day by day be molded upon Thee, and be changed from glory to glory, by ever looking towards Thee, and ever leaning on Thy arm. I know, O Lord, I must go through trial, temptation, and much conflict, if I am to come to Thee. I know not what lies before me, but I know as much as this. I know, too, that if Thou art not with me, my change will be for the worse, not for the better. Whatever fortune I have, be I rich or poor, healthy or sick, with friends or without, all will turn to evil if I am not sustained by the Unchangeable; all will turn to good if I have Jesus with me, yesterday and today the same, and forever.

X

GOD IS LOVE

"Jesus saith to him, Lovest thou Me more than these?"
(JOHN 21:15)

1. Thou askest us to love Thee, O my God, and Thou art Thyself
   Love. There was one attribute of Thine which Thou didst exercise
   from eternity, and that was Love. We hear of no exercise of Thy
   power whilst Thou wast alone, nor of Thy justice before there were
   creatures on their trial; nor of Thy wisdom before the acts and
   works of Thy Providence; but from eternity Thou didst love, for
   Thou art not only One but Three. The Father loved from eternity
   His only begotten Son, and the Son returned to Him an equal
   love. And the Holy Ghost is that love in substance, wherewith
   the Father and the Son love one another. This, O Lord, is Thine
   ineffable and special blessedness. It is love. I adore Thee, O my
   infinite Love!

2. And when Thou hadst created us, then Thou didst but love more,
   if that were possible. Thou didst love not only Thy own Co-equal
   Self in the multiplied Personality of the Godhead, but Thou didst
   love Thy creatures also. Thou wast love to us, as well as Love in
   Thyself. Thou wast love to man, more than to any other creatures.
   It was love that brought Thee from heaven, and subjected Thee to
   the laws of a created nature. It was love alone which was able to
   conquer Thee, the Highest—and bring Thee low. Thou didst die
   through Thine infinite love of sinners. And it is love, which keeps
   Thee here still, even now that Thou hast ascended on high, in a
   small tabernacle, and under cheap and common outward forms. *O
   Amor meus,* if Thou wert not infinite Love, wouldest Thou remain
   here, one hour, imprisoned and exposed to slight, indignity, and

THREE *Meditations on Christian Doctrine* | 157

insult? O my God, I do not know what infinity means—but one thing I see, that Thou art loving to a depth and height far beyond any measurement of mine.

3.   And now Thou biddest me love Thee in turn, for Thou hast loved me. Thou wooest me to love Thee specially, above others. Thou dost say, "Lovest thou Me more than these?" (John 21:15). O my God, how shameful that such a question need be put to me! yet, after all, do I really love Thee more than the run of men? The run of men do not really love Thee at all, but put Thee out of their thoughts. They feel it unpleasant to them to think of Thee; they have no sort of heart for Thee, yet Thou hast need to ask me whether I love Thee even a little. Why should I not love Thee much, how can I help loving Thee much, whom Thou hast brought so near to Thyself, whom Thou hast so wonderfully chosen out of the world to be Thy own special servant and son? Have I not cause to love Thee abundantly more than others, though all ought to love Thee? I do not know what Thou hast done for others personally, though Thou hast died for all—but I know what Thou hast done specially for me. Thou hast done that for me, O my love, which ought to make me love Thee with all my powers.

XI
THE SANCTITY OF GOD

1.   Thou art holy, O Lord, in that Thou art infinitely separate from everything but Thyself, and incommunicable. I adore Thee, O Lord, in this Thy proper sanctity and everlasting purity, for that all Thy blessedness comes from within, and nothing touches Thee from without. I adore Thee as infinitely blessed, yet having all Thy blessedness in Thyself. I adore Thee in that perfect and most holy

knowledge of Thyself, in which we conceive the generation of the Word. I adore Thee in that infinite and most pure love of Thyself, a love of Thy Son, and Thy Son's love for Thee, in which we conceive the procession of the Holy Ghost. I adore Thee in that blessedness which Thou didst possess in Thyself from all eternity. My God, I do not understand these heavenly things. I use words which I cannot master; but I believe, O God, that to be true, which I thus feebly express in human language.

2. My God, I adore Thee, as holy without, as well as holy within. I adore Thee as holy in all Thy works as well as in Thy own nature. No creature can approach Thy incommunicable sanctity, but Thou dost approach, and touch, and compass, and possess, all creatures; and nothing lives but in Thee, and nothing hast Thou created but what is good. I adore Thee, as having made everything good after its kind. I adore Thee, as having infused Thy preserving and sustaining power into all things, while Thou didst create them, so that they continue to live, though Thou dost not touch them, and do not crumble back into nothing. I adore Thee, as having put real power into them, so that they are able to act, although from Thee and with Thee and yet of themselves. I adore Thee as having given power to will what is right, and Thy holy grace to Thy rational creatures. I adore Thee as having created man upright, and having bountifully given him an integrity of nature, and having filled him with Thy free grace, so that he was like an Angel upon earth; and I adore Thee still more, for having given him Thy grace over again in still more copious measure, and with far more lasting fruits, through Thy Eternal Son incarnate. In all Thy works Thou art holy, O my God, and I adore Thee in them all.

3. Holy art Thou in all Thy works, O Lord, and, if there is sin in the world it is not from Thee—it is from an enemy, it is from me

and mine. To me, to man, be the shame, for we might will what is right, and we will what is evil. What a gulf is there between Thee and me, O my Creator—not only as to nature but as to will! Thy will is ever holy; how, O Lord, shall I ever dare approach Thee? What have I to do with Thee? Yet I must approach Thee; Thou wilt call me to Thee when I die, and judge me. Woe is me, for I am a man of unclean lips, and dwell in the midst of a people of unclean lips! Thy Cross, O Lord, shows the distance that is between Thee and me, while it takes it away. It shows both my great sinfulness and Thy utter abhorrence of sin. Impart to me, my dear Lord, the doctrine of the Cross in its fullness, that it may not only teach me my alienation from Thee, but convey to me the virtue of Thy reconciliation.

XII
THE FORTY DAYS' TEACHING

The Kingdom of God

1. My Lord Jesus, how wonderful were those conversations which Thou didst hold from time to time with Thy disciples after Thy resurrection. When Thou wentest with two of them to Emmaus, Thou didst explain all the prophecies which related to Thyself. And Thou didst commit to the Apostles the Sacraments in fullness, and the truths which it was Thy will to reveal, and the principles and maxims by which Thy Church was to be maintained and governed. And thus, Thou didst prepare them against the day of Pentecost (as the risen bodies were put into shape for the Spirit in the Prophet's Vision), when life and illumination was to be infused into them. I will think over all Thou didst say to them with a true and simple faith. The "kingdom of God" was Thy sacred subject. Let me never

for an instant forget that Thou hast established on earth a kingdom of Thy own, that the Church is Thy work, Thy establishment, Thy instrument; that we are under Thy rule, Thy laws and Thy eye— that when the Church speaks Thou dost speak. Let not familiarity with this wonderful truth lead me to be insensible to it—let not the weakness of Thy human representatives lead me to forget that it is Thou who dost speak and act through them. It was just when Thou wast going away, that then Thou didst leave this kingdom of Thine to take Thy place on to the end of the world, to speak for Thee, as Thy visible form, when Thy Personal Presence, sensible to man, was departing. I will in true loving faith bring Thee before me, teaching all the truths and laws of this kingdom to Thy Apostles, and I will adore Thee, while in my thoughts I gaze upon Thee and listen to Thy words.

2. Come, O my dear Lord, and teach me in like manner. I need it not, and do not ask it, as far as this, that the word of truth which in the beginning was given to the Apostles by Thee, has been handed down from age to age, and has already been taught to me, and Thy Infallible Church is the warrant of it. But I need Thee to teach me day by day, according to each day's opportunities and needs. I need Thee to give me that true Divine instinct about revealed matters that, knowing one part, I may be able to anticipate or to approve of others. I need that understanding of the truths about Thyself which may prepare me for all Thy other truths—or at least may save me from conjecturing wrongly about them or commenting falsely upon them. I need the mind of the Spirit, which is the mind of the holy Fathers, and of the Church by which I may not only say what they say on definite points, but think what they think; in all I need to be saved from an originality of thought, which is not true if it leads away from Thee. Give me the gift of discriminating between true and false in all discourse of mind.

3. And, for that end, give me, O my Lord, that purity of conscience which alone can receive, which alone can improve Thy inspirations. My ears are dull, so that I cannot hear Thy voice. My eyes are dim, so that I cannot see Thy tokens. Thou alone canst quicken my hearing, and purge my sight, and cleanse and renew my heart. Teach me, like Mary, to sit at Thy feet, and to hear Thy word. Give me that true wisdom, which seeks Thy will by prayer and meditation, by direct intercourse with Thee, more than by reading and reasoning. Give me the discernment to know Thy voice from the voice of strangers, and to rest upon it and to seek it in the first place, as something external to myself; and answer me through my own mind, if I worship and rely on Thee as above and beyond it.

Resignation to God's Will

"What is it to thee? Follow thou Me." (JOHN 21:22)

1. O my God, Thou and Thou alone art all-wise and all-knowing! Thou knowest, Thou hast determined everything which will happen to us from first to last. Thou hast ordered things in the wisest way, and Thou knowest what will be my lot year by year till I die. Thou knowest how long I have to live. Thou knowest how I shall die. Thou hast precisely ordained everything, sin excepted. Every event of my life is the best for me that could be, for it comes from Thee. Thou dost bring me on year by year, by Thy wonderful Providence, from youth to age, with the most perfect wisdom, and with the most perfect love.

2 My Lord, who camest into this world to do Thy Father's will, not Thine own, give me a most absolute and simple submission to the will of Father and Son. I believe, O my Savior, that Thou knowest

just what is best for me. I believe that Thou lovest me better than
I love myself, that Thou art all-wise in Thy Providence, and all-
powerful in Thy protection. I am as ignorant as Peter was what is
to happen to me in time to come; but I resign myself entirely to
my ignorance, and thank Thee with all my heart that Thou hast
taken me out of my own keeping, and, instead of putting such
a serious charge upon me, hast bidden me put myself into Thy
hands. I can ask nothing better than this, to be Thy care, not my
own. I protest, O my Lord, that, through Thy grace, I will follow
Thee whithersoever Thou goest, and will not lead the way. I will
wait on Thee for Thy guidance, and, on obtaining it, I will act
upon it in simplicity and without fear. And I promise that I will
not be impatient, if at any time I am kept by Thee in darkness
and perplexity; nor will I ever complain or fret if I come into any
misfortune or anxiety.

3. I know, O Lord, Thou wilt do Thy part towards me, as I, through
    Thy grace, desire to do my part towards Thee. I know well Thou
    never canst forsake those who seek Thee, or canst disappoint
    those who trust Thee. Yet I know too, the more I pray for Thy
    protection, the more surely and fully I shall have it. And therefore,
    now I cry out to Thee, and entreat Thee, first that Thou wouldest
    keep me from myself, and from following any will but Thine. Next
    I beg of Thee, that in Thy infinite compassion, Thou wouldest
    temper Thy will to me, that it may not be severe, but indulgent
    to me. Visit me not, O my loving Lord—if it be not wrong so
    to pray—visit me not with those trying visitations which saints
    alone can bear! Pity my weakness, and lead me heavenwards in
    a safe and tranquil course. Still I leave all in Thy hands, my dear
    Savior—I bargain for nothing—only, if Thou shalt bring heavier
    trials on me, give me more grace—flood me with the fullness
    of Thy strength and consolation, that they may work in me not
    death, but life and salvation.

Our Lord's Parting with His Apostles

1. I adore Thee, O my God! together with Thy Apostles, during the forty days in which Thou didst visit them after Thy resurrection. So blessed was the time, so calm, so undisturbed from without, that it was good to be there with Thee, and when it was over, they could hardly believe that it was more than begun. How quickly must that first *Tempus Paschale* [Easter Season] have flown! and they perhaps hardly knew when it was to end. At least, they did not like to anticipate its ending, but were engrossed with the joy of the present moment. O what a time of consolation! What a contrast to what had lately taken place! It was their happy time on earth—the foretaste of heaven; not noticed, not interfered with, by man. They passed it in wonder, in musing, in adoration, rejoicing in Thy light, O my risen God!

2. But Thou, O my dear Lord, didst know better than they! They hoped and desired, perhaps fancied, that that resting time, that *refrigerium* [refreshment], never would end till it was superseded by something better; but Thou didst know, in Thy eternal wisdom, that, in order to arrive at what was higher than any blessing which they were then enjoying, it was fitting, it was necessary, that they should sustain conflict and suffering. Thou knewest well, that unless Thou hadst departed, the Paraclete could not have come to them; and therefore, Thou didst go, that they might gain more by Thy sorrowful absence than by Thy sensible visitations. I adore Thee, O Father, for sending the Son and the Holy Ghost! I adore Thee, O Son, and Thee, O Holy Ghost, for vouchsafing to be sent to us!

3. O my God, let me never forget that seasons of consolation are refreshments here, and nothing more; not our abiding state. They will not remain with us except in heaven. Here they are only

intended to prepare us for doing and suffering. I pray Thee, O my God, to give them to me from time to time. Shed over me the sweetness of Thy Presence, lest I faint by the way; lest I find religious service wearisome, through my exceeding infirmity, and give over prayer and meditation; lest I go about my daily work in a dry spirit, or am tempted to take pleasure in it for its own sake, and not for Thee. Give me Thy Divine consolations from time to time; but let me not rest in them. Let me use them for the purpose for which Thou givest them. Let me not think it grievous, let me not be downcast, if they go. Let them carry me forward to the thought and the desire of heaven.

God's Ways Not Our Ways

"Because I have spoken these things to you, sorrow hath filled your heart. But I tell you the truth: it is expedient for you." (JOHN 16:6)

1. O my Savior, I adore Thee for Thy infinite wisdom, which sees what we do not see, and orderest all things in its own most perfect way. When Thou didst say to the Apostles that Thou wast going away, they cried out, as if Thou hadst, if it may be so said, broken faith with them. They seemed to say to Thee, "O Jesu, did we not leave all things for Thee? Did we not give up home and family, father and wife, friends and neighbors, our habits, our accustomed way of living, that we might join Thee? Did we not divorce ourselves from the world, or rather die to it, that we might be eternally united and live to Thee? And now Thou sayest that Thou art leaving us. Is this reasonable? is this just? is this faithfulness to Thy promise? Did we bargain for this? O Lord Jesus, we adore Thee, but we are confounded, and we know not what to say!"

2. Yet let God be true, and every man a liar. Let the Divine Word triumph in our minds over every argument and persuasion of sensible appearances. Let faith rule us and not sight. Thou art justified, O Lord, when Thou art arraigned, and dost gain the cause when Thou art judged. For Thou didst know that the true way of possessing Thee was to lose Thee. Thou didst know that what man stands most of all in need of, and in the first place, is not an outward guide, though that he needs too, but an inward, intimate, invisible aid. Thou didst intend to heal him thoroughly, not slightly; not merely to reform the surface, but to remove and destroy the heart and root of all his ills. Thou then didst purpose to visit his soul, and Thou didst depart in body, that Thou mightest come again to him in spirit. Thou didst not stay with Thy Apostles therefore, as in the days of Thy flesh, but Thou didst come to them and abide with them forever, with a much more immediate and true communion in the power of the Paraclete.

3. O my God, in Thy sight, I confess and bewail my extreme weakness, in distrusting, if not Thee, at least Thy own servants and representatives, when things do not turn out as I would have them, or expected! Thou hast given me St. Philip, that great creation of Thy grace, for my master and patron—and I have committed myself to him—and he has done very great things for me, and has in many ways fulfilled towards me all that I can fairly reckon he had promised. But, because in some things he has disappointed me, and delayed, I have got impatient; and have served him, though without conscious disloyalty, yet with peevishness and coldness. O my dear Lord, give me a generous faith in Thee and in Thy servants!

XIII
THE ASCENSION

He Ascended

1. My Lord, I follow Thee up to heaven; as Thou goest up, my heart and mind go with Thee. Never was triumph like this. Thou didst appear a babe in human flesh at Bethlehem. That flesh, taken from the Blessed Virgin, was not before Thou didst form it into a body; it was a new work of Thy hands. And Thy soul was new altogether, created by Thy Omnipotence, at the moment when Thou didst enter into her sacred breast. That pure soul and body, taken as a garment for Thyself, began on earth, and never had been elsewhere. This is the triumph. Earth rises to heaven. I see Thee going up. I see that Form which hung upon the Cross, those scarred hands and feet, that pierced side; they are mounting up to heaven. And the Angels are full of jubilee; the myriads of blessed spirits, which people the glorious expanse, part like the waters to let Thee pass. And the living pavement of God's palaces is cleft in twain, and the Cherubim with flaming swords, who form the rampart of heaven against fallen man, give way and open out, that Thou mayest enter, and Thy saints after Thee. O memorable day!

2. O memorable day! The Apostles feel it to be so, now that it is come, though they felt so differently before it came. When it was coming, they dreaded it. They could not think but it would be a great bereavement; but now, as we read, they returned to Jerusalem "with great joy" (Luke 24:52). O what a time of triumph! They understood it now. They understood how weak it had been in them to grudge their Lord and Master, the glorious Captain of their salvation, the Champion and First fruits of the human family, this crown of His great work. It was the triumph of redeemed

man. It is the completion of his redemption. It was the last act, making the whole sure, for now man is actually in heaven. He has entered into possession of his inheritance. The sinful race has now one of its own children there, its own flesh and blood, in the person of the Eternal Son. O what a wonderful marriage between heaven and earth! It began in sorrow; but now the long travail of that mysterious wedding day is over; the marriage feast is begun; marriage and birth have gone together; man is new born when Emmanuel enters heaven.

3. O Emmanuel, O God in our flesh! we too hope, by Thy grace, to follow Thee. We will cling to the skirts of Thy garments, as Thou goest up; for without Thee we cannot ascend. O Emmanuel, what a day of joy when we shall enter heaven! O inexpressible ecstasy, after all trouble! There is none strong but Thou. *Tenuisti manum dexteram meam: et in voluntate tua deduxisti me, et cum gloria suscepisti me. Quid enim mihi est in cœlo, et a Te quid volui super terram? Defecit caro mea et cor meum; Deus cordis mei, et pars mea Deus in æternum.*—"Thou hast held me by my right hand; and by Thy will Thou hast conducted me, and with Thy glory Thou hast received me. For what have I in heaven? And besides Thee what do I desire upon earth? For Thee my flesh and my heart hath fainted away: Thou art the God of my heart, and the God that is my portion forever" (Psalm 73:24–25).

Ascendit in Cœlum, He Ascended into Heaven

1. My Lord is gone up into heaven. I adore Thee, Son of Mary, Jesu Emmanuel, my God and my Savior. I am allowed to adore Thee, my Savior and my own Brother, for Thou art God. I follow Thee

in my thoughts, O Thou First fruits of our race, as I hope one day by Thy grace to follow Thee in my person. To go to heaven is to go to God. God is there and God alone: for perfect bliss is there and nothing else, and none can be blessed who is not bathed and hidden and absorbed in the glory of the Divine Nature. All holy creatures are but the vestment of the Highest, which He has put on forever, and which is bright with His uncreated light. There are many things on earth, and each is its own center, but one Name alone is named above. It is God alone. This is that true supernatural life; and if I would live a supernatural life on earth, and attain to the supernatural eternal life which is in heaven, I have one thing to do, namely, to live on the thought of God here. Teach me this, O God; give me Thy supernatural grace to practice it; to have my reason, affections, intentions, aims, all penetrated and possessed by the love of Thee, plunged and drowned in the one Vision of Thee.

2. There is but one Name and one Thought above: there are many thoughts below. This is the earthly life, which leads to death, in other words, to follow the numberless objects and aims and toils and amusements which men pursue on earth. Even the good that is here below does not lead to heaven; it is spoilt in the handselling; it perishes in the using; it has no stay, no integrity, no consistency. It runs off into evil before it has well ceased, before it has well begun to be good. It is at best vanity, when it is nothing worse. It has in it commonly the seeds of real sin. My God, I acknowledge all this. My Lord Jesu, I confess and know that Thou only art the True, the Beautiful, and the Good. Thou alone canst make me bright and glorious, and canst lead me up after Thee. Thou art the way, the truth, and the life, and none but Thou. Earth will never lead me to heaven. Thou alone art the Way; Thou alone.

3. My God, shall I for one moment doubt where my path lies? Shall I not at once take Thee for my portion? To whom should I go? Thou hast the words of Eternal Life. Thou camest down for the very purpose of doing that which no one here below could do for me. None but He who is in heaven can bring me to heaven. What strength have I to scale the high mountain? Though I served the world ever so well, though I did my duty in it (as men speak), what could the world do for me, however hard it tried? Though I filled my station well, did good to my fellows, had a fair name or a wide reputation, though I did great deeds and was celebrated, though I had the praise of history, how would all this bring me to heaven? I choose Thee then for my One Portion, because Thou livest and diest not. I cast away all idols. I give myself to Thee. I pray Thee to teach me, guide me, enable me, and receive me to Thee.

Our Advocate Above

1. I adore Thee, O my Lord, as is most fitting, for Thou art gone to heaven to take my part there, and defend my interests. I have one to plead for me with the Lord of all. On earth, we try to put ourselves under the protection of powerful men when we have any important business on hand; we know the value of their influence, and we make much of any promise they make us. Thou art omnipotent, and Thou dost exert Thy omnipotence for me. There are millions of men in the world: thou didst die for them all; but Thou livest for Thy people, whom Thou hast chosen out of the world. And still more marvelously dost Thou live for Thy predestinate. Thou hast engraven them upon the palms of Thy hands; their names are ever before Thee. Thou countest the full roll of them; Thou knowest them by heart: Thou orderest the crown of the world for them; and, when their number shall be completed, the world shall end.

2. For me, Thou hast chosen me for present grace—and thus Thou hast put me in the way for future glory. I know perfectly well that, whatever be Thy secret counsels about me, it will be simply, entirely, most really my own fault if I am not written in Thy book. I cannot understand Thee: I can understand myself enough to know and be sure of this. Thou hast put me on such especial vantage ground that the prize is almost in my hand. If I am at present in the society of Angels or Saints, it is hard if I cannot make interest with them that the fellowship begun between them and me should endure. Men of the world know how to turn such opportunities to account in their own matters. If Thou hast given me Mary for my Mother, who, O my God! is Thine, cannot I now establish, as it were, a family interest in her, so that she will not cast me off at the last? If I have the right to pray and the gift of impetration, may I not thereby secure that perseverance to the end, which I cannot merit, and which is the sign and assurance of my predestination? I have in my hands all the means of that which I have not, and may infallibly obtain, even though I cannot certainly secure it.

3. O my Lord, I sink down almost in despair, in utter remorse certainly and disgust at myself, that I so utterly neglect these means which Thou hast put into my hands, content to let things take their course, as if grace would infallibly lead to glory without my own trouble in the matter. What shall I say to Thee, O my Savior! except that I am in the chains of habit, feeble, helpless, stunted, growthless, and as if I were meant to walk through life, as the inferior creatures, with my face down to the earth, on hands and feet, or crawling on, instead of having an erect posture and a heavenward face? O give me what I need—contrition for all those infinitely numerous venial sins, negligences, slovenliness, which are the surest foreboding that I am not of Thy predestinate. Who can save me from myself but Thou?

Our Advocate Above

1. I cannot penetrate Thy secret decrees, O Lord! I know Thou didst die for all men really; but since thou hast not effectually willed the salvation of all, and since Thou mightest have done so, it is certain that Thou doest for one what Thou dost not do for another. I cannot tell what has been Thy everlasting purpose about myself, but, if I go by all the signs which Thou hast lavished upon me, I may hope that I am one of those whose names are written in Thy book. But this I know and feel most entirely, what I believe in the case of all men, but know and feel in my own case, that, if I do not attain to that crown which I see and which is within my reach, it is entirely my own fault. Thou hast surrounded me from childhood with Thy mercies; Thou hast taken as much pains with me as if I was of importance to Thee, and my loss of heaven would be Thy loss of me. Thou hast led me on by ten thousand merciful providences; Thou hast brought me near to Thee in the most intimate of ways; Thou hast brought me into Thy house and chamber; Thou hast fed me with Thyself. Dost Thou not love me? really, truly, substantially, efficaciously love me, without any limitation of the word? I know it. I have an utter conviction of it. Thou art ever waiting to do me benefits, to pour upon me blessings. Thou art ever waiting for me to ask Thee to be merciful to me.

2. Yes, my Lord, Thou dost desire that I should ask Thee; Thou art ever listening for my voice. There is nothing I cannot get from Thee. Oh, I confess my heinous neglect of this great privilege. I am very guilty. I have trifled with the highest of gifts, the power to move Omnipotence. How slack am I in praying to Thee for my own needs! how little have I thought of the needs of others! How little have I brought before Thee the needs of the world—of Thy Church! How little I have asked for graces in detail! and for aid in

daily wants! How little have I interceded for individuals! How little have I accompanied actions and undertakings, in themselves good, with prayer for Thy guidance and blessing!

3. O my Lord Jesu, I will use the time. It will be too late to pray, when life is over. There is no prayer in the grave—there is no meriting in Purgatory. Low as I am in Thy all holy sight, I am strong in Thee, strong through Thy Immaculate Mother, through Thy Saints: and thus, I can do much for the Church, for the world, for all I love. O let not the blood of souls be on my head! O let me not walk my own way without thinking of Thee. Let me bring everything before Thee, asking Thy leave for everything I purpose, Thy blessing on everything I do. I will not move without Thee. I will ever lift up my heart to Thee. I will never forget that Thou art my Advocate at the Throne of the Highest. As the dial speaks of the sun, so will I be ruled by Thee above, if Thou wilt take me and rule me. Be it so, my Lord Jesus. I give myself wholly to Thee.

XIV
THE PARACLETE

The Paraclete, the Life of all Things

1. I adore Thee, my Lord and God, the Eternal Paraclete, co-equal with the Father and the Son. I adore Thee as the Life of all that live. Through Thee the whole material Universe hangs together and consists, remains in its place, and moves internally in the order and reciprocity of its several parts. Through Thee the earth was brought into its present state, and was matured through its six days to be a habitation for man. Through Thee, all trees, herbs, fruits, thrive and are perfected. Through Thee, spring comes after winter and renews all things. That wonderful and beautiful, that

irresistible burst into life again, in spite of all obstacles, that awful triumph of nature, is but Thy glorious Presence. Through Thee the many tribes of brute animals live day by day, drawing in their breath from Thee. Thou art the life of the whole creation, O Eternal Paraclete—and if of this animal and material framework, how much more of the world of spirits! Through Thee, Almighty Lord, the angels and saints sing Thee praises in heaven. Through Thee our own dead souls are quickened to serve Thee. From Thee is every good thought and desire, every good purpose, every good effort, every good success. It is by Thee that sinners are turned into saints. It is by Thee the Church is refreshed and strengthened, and champions start forth, and martyrs are carried on to their crown. Through Thee new religious orders, new devotions in the Church come into being; new countries are added to the faith, new manifestations and illustrations are given to the ancient Apostolic creed. I praise and adore Thee, my Sovereign Lord God, the Holy Ghost.

2. I adore Thee, O dread Lord, for what Thou hast done for my soul. I acknowledge and feel, not only as a matter of faith but of experience, that I cannot have one good thought or do one good act without Thee. I know, that if I attempt anything good in my own strength, I shall to a certainty fail. I have bitter experience of this. My God, I am only safe when Thou dost breathe upon me. If Thou withdraw Thy breath, forthwith my three mortal enemies rush on me and overcome me. I am as weak as water, I am utterly impotent without Thee. The minute Thou dost cease to act in me, I begin to languish, to gasp, and to faint away. Of my good desires, whatever they may be, of my good aims, aspirations, attempts, successes, habits, practices, Thou art the sole cause and present continual source. I have nothing but what I have received, and I protest now in Thy presence, O Sovereign Paraclete, that I have nothing to glory in, and everything to be humbled at.

3. O my dear Lord, how merciful Thou hast been to me. When I was young, Thou didst put into my heart a special devotion to Thee. Thou hast taken me up in my youth, and in my age Thou wilt not forsake me. Not for my merit, but from Thy free and bountiful love Thou didst put good resolutions into me when I was young, and didst turn me to Thee. Thou wilt never forsake me. I do earnestly trust so—never certainly without fearful provocation on my part. Yet I trust and pray, that Thou wilt keep me from that provocation. O keep me from the provocation of lukewarmness and sloth. O my dear Lord, lead me forward from strength to strength, gently, sweetly, tenderly, lovingly, powerfully, effectually, remembering my fretfulness and feebleness, till Thou bringest me into Thy heaven.

The Paraclete, the Life of the Church

1. I adore Thee, O my Lord, the Third Person of the All-Blessed Trinity, that Thou hast set up in this world of sin a great light upon a hill. Thou hast founded the Church, Thou hast established and maintained it. Thou fillest it continually with Thy gifts, that men may see, and draw near, and take, and live. Thou hast in this way brought down heaven upon earth. For Thou hast set up a great company which Angels visit by that ladder which the Patriarch saw in vision. Thou hast by Thy Presence restored the communion between God above and man below. Thou hast given him that light of grace which is one with and the commencement of the light of glory. I adore and praise Thee for Thy infinite mercy towards us, O my Lord and God.

2. I adore Thee, O Almighty Lord, the Paraclete, because Thou in Thy infinite compassion hast brought me into this Church, the work of Thy supernatural power. I had no claim on Thee for so wonderful

a favor over anyone else in the whole world. There were many men far better than I by nature, gifted with more pleasing natural gifts, and less stained with sin. Yet Thou, in Thy inscrutable love for me, hast chosen me and brought me into Thy fold. Thou hast a reason for everything Thou dost. I know there must have been an all-wise reason, as we speak in human language, for Thy choosing me and not another—but I know that that reason was something external to myself. I did nothing towards it—I did everything against it. I did everything to thwart Thy purpose. And thus, I owe all to Thy grace. I should have lived and died in darkness and sin; I should have become worse and worse the longer I lived; I should have got more to hate and abjure Thee, O Source of my bliss; I should have got yearly more fit for hell, and at length I should have gone there, but for Thy incomprehensible love to me. O my God, that overpowering love took me captive. Was any boyhood so impious as some years of mine! Did I not in fact dare Thee to do Thy worst? Ah, how I struggled to get free from Thee; but Thou art stronger than I and hast prevailed. I have not a word to say, but to bow down in awe before the depths of Thy love.

3.   And then, in course of time, slowly but infallibly did Thy grace bring me on into Thy Church. Now then give me this further grace, Lord, to use all this grace well, and to turn it to my salvation. Teach me, make me, to come to the fountains of mercy continually with an awakened, eager mind, and with lively devotion. Give me a love of Thy Sacraments and Ordinances. Teach me to value as I ought, to prize as the inestimable pearl, that pardon which again and again Thou givest me, and the great and heavenly gift of the Presence of Him whose Spirit Thou art, upon the Altar. Without Thee I can do nothing, and Thou art there where Thy Church is and Thy Sacraments. Give me grace to rest in them forever, till they are lost in the glory of Thy manifestation in the world to come.

The Paraclete, the Life of my Soul

1. My God, I adore Thee for taking on Thee the charge of sinners; of those, who not only cannot profit Thee, but who continually grieve and profane Thee. Thou hast taken on Thyself the office of a minister, and that for those who did not ask for it. I adore Thee for Thy incomprehensible condescension in ministering to me. I know and feel, O my God, that Thou mightest have left me, as I wished to be left, to go my own way, to go straight forward in my willfulness and self-trust to hell. Thou mightest have left me in that enmity to Thee which is in itself death. I should at length have died the second death, and should have had no one to blame for it but myself. But Thou, O Eternal Father, hast been kinder to me than I am to myself. Thou hast given me, Thou hast poured out upon me Thy grace, and thus I live.

2. My God, I adore Thee, O Eternal Paraclete, the light and the life of my soul. Thou mightest have been content with merely giving me good suggestions, inspiring grace and helping from without. Thou mightest thus have led me on, cleansing me with Thy inward virtue, when I changed my state from this world to the next. But in Thine infinite compassion Thou hast from the first entered into my soul, and taken possession of it. Thou hast made it Thy Temple. Thou dwellest in me by Thy grace in an ineffable way, uniting me to Thyself and the whole company of angels and saints. Nay, as some have held, Thou art present in me, not only by Thy grace, but by Thy eternal substance, as if, though I did not lose my own individuality, yet in some sense I was even here absorbed in God. Nay—as though Thou hadst taken possession of my very body, this earthly, fleshly, wretched tabernacle—even my body is Thy Temple. O astonishing, awful truth! I believe it, I know it, O my God!

3. O my God, can I sin when Thou art so intimately with me? Can I forget who is with me, who is in me? Can I expel a Divine Inhabitant by that which He abhors more than anything else, which is the one thing in the whole world which is offensive to Him, the only thing which is not His? Would not this be a kind of sin against the Holy Ghost? My God, I have a double security against sinning; first the dread of such a profanation of all Thou art to me in Thy very Presence; and next because I do trust that that Presence will preserve me from sin. My God, Thou wilt go from me, if I sin; and I shall be left to my own miserable self. God forbid! I will use what Thou hast given me; I will call on Thee when tried and tempted. I will guard against the sloth and carelessness into which I am continually falling. Through Thee I will never forsake Thee.

The Paraclete, the Fount of Love

1. My God, I adore Thee, as the Third Person of the Ever-Blessed Trinity, under the name and designation of Love. Thou art that Living Love, wherewith the Father and the Son love each other. And Thou art the Author of supernatural love in our hearts—"*Fons vivus, ignis, caritas.*" As a fire, Thou didst come down from heaven on the day of Pentecost; and as a fire Thou burnest away the dross of sin and vanity in the heart and dost light up the pure flame of devotion and affection. It is Thou who unitest heaven and earth by showing to us the glory and beauty of the Divine Nature, and making us love what is in Itself so winning and transporting. I adore Thee, O uncreate and everlasting Fire, by which our souls live, by which alone they are made fit for heaven.

2. My God, the Paraclete, I acknowledge Thee as the Giver of that great gift, by which alone we are saved, supernatural love. Man is by nature blind and hardhearted in all spiritual matters; how is he to reach heaven? It is by the flame of Thy grace, which consumes him in order to new-make him, and so to fit him to enjoy what without Thee he would have no taste for. It is Thou, O Almighty Paraclete, who hast been and art the strength, the vigor and endurance, of the martyr in the midst of his torments. Thou art the stay of the confessor in his long, tedious, and humiliating toils. Thou art the fire, by which the preacher wins souls, without thought of himself, in his missionary labors. By Thee we wake up from the death of sin, to exchange the idolatry of the creature for the pure love of the Creator. By Thee we make acts of faith, hope, charity, and contrition. By Thee we live in the atmosphere of earth, proof against its infection. By Thee we are able to consecrate ourselves to the sacred ministry, and fulfil our awful engagements to it. By the fire which Thou didst kindle within us, we pray, and meditate, and do penance. As well could our bodies live, if the sun were extinguished, as our souls, if Thou art away.

3 My most Holy Lord and Sanctifier, whatever there is of good in me is Thine. Without Thee, I should but get worse and worse as years went on, and should tend to be a devil. If I differ at all from the world, it is because Thou hast chosen me out of the world, and hast lit up the love of God in my heart. If I differ from Thy Saints, it is because I do not ask earnestly enough for Thy grace, and for enough of it, and because I do not diligently improve what Thou hast given me. Increase in me this grace of love, in spite of all my unworthiness. It is more precious than anything else in the world. I accept it in place of all the world can give me. O give it to me! It is my life.

XV
THE HOLY SACRIFICE

The Mass

1. I adore Thee, O my Lord God, with the most profound awe for thy passion and crucifixion, in sacrifice for our sins. Thou didst suffer incommunicable sufferings in Thy sinless soul. Thou wast exposed in Thy innocent body to ignominious torments, to mingled pain and shame. Thou wast stripped and fiercely scourged, Thy sacred body vibrating under the heavy flail as trees under the blast. Thou wast, when thus mangled, hung up upon the Cross, naked, a spectacle for all to see Thee quivering and dying. What does all this imply, O Mighty God! What a depth is here which we cannot fathom! My God, I know well, Thou couldst have saved us at Thy word, without Thyself suffering; but Thou didst choose to purchase us at the price of Thy Blood. I look on Thee, the Victim lifted up on Calvary, and I know and protest that that death of Thine was an expiation for the sins of the whole world. I believe and know, that Thou alone couldst have offered a meritorious atonement; for it was Thy Divine Nature which gave Thy sufferings worth. Rather then than I should perish according to my deserts, Thou wast nailed to the Tree and didst die.

2. Such a sacrifice was not to be forgotten. It was not to be—it could not be—a mere event in the world's history, which was to be done and over, and was to pass away except in its obscure, unrecognized effects. If that great deed was what we believe it to be, what we know it is, it must remain present, though past; it must be a standing fact for all times. Our own careful reflection upon it tells us this; and therefore, when we are told that Thou, O Lord, though Thou hast ascended to glory, hast renewed and perpetuated Thy sacrifice to the end of all things, not only is the news most touching and joyful,

as testifying to so tender a Lord and Savior, but it carries with it the full assent and sympathy of our reason. Though we neither could, nor would have dared, anticipate so wonderful a doctrine, yet we adore its very suitableness to Thy perfections, as well as its infinite compassionateness for us, now that we are told of it. Yes, my Lord, though Thou hast left the world, Thou art daily offered up in the Mass; and, though Thou canst not suffer pain and death, Thou dost still subject Thyself to indignity and restraint to carry out to the full Thy mercies towards us. Thou dost humble Thyself daily; for, being infinite, Thou couldst not end Thy humiliation while they existed for whom Thou didst submit to it. So, Thou remainest a Priest forever.

3. My Lord, I offer Thee myself in turn as a sacrifice of thanksgiving. Thou hast died for me, and I in turn make myself over to Thee. I am not my own. Thou hast bought me; I will by my own act and deed complete the purchase. My wish is to be separated from everything of this world; to cleanse myself simply from sin; to put away from me even what is innocent, if used for its own sake, and not for Thine. I put away reputation and honor, and influence, and power, for my praise and strength shall be in Thee. Enable me to carry out what I profess.

Holy Communion

1. My God, who can be inhabited by Thee, except the pure and holy? Sinners may come to Thee, but to whom shouldst Thou come except to the sanctified? My God, I adore Thee as the Holiest; and, when Thou didst come upon earth, Thou didst prepare a holy habitation for Thyself in the most chaste womb of the Blessed Virgin. Thou didst make a dwelling place special for Thyself. She did not receive Thee without first being prepared for Thee; for

from the moment that she was at all, she was filled with Thy grace, so that she never knew sin. And so, she went on increasing in grace and merit year after year, till the time came, when Thou didst send down the Archangel to signify to her Thy presence within her. So holy must be the dwelling place of the Highest. I adore and glorify Thee, O Lord my God, for Thy great holiness.

2.   O my God, holiness becometh Thy House, and yet Thou dost make Thy abode in my breast. My Lord, my Savior, to me Thou comest, hidden under the semblance of earthly things, yet in that very flesh and blood which Thou didst take from Mary. Thou, who didst first inhabit Mary's breast, dost come to me. My God, Thou seest me; I cannot see myself. Were I ever so good a judge about myself, ever so unbiased, and with ever so correct a rule of judging, still, from my very nature, I cannot look at myself, and view myself truly and wholly. But Thou, as Thou comest to me, contemplatest me. When I say, *Domine, non sum dignus*—"Lord, I am not worthy" (Matthew 8:8)—Thou whom I am addressing, alone understandest in their fullness the words which I use. Thou seest how unworthy so great a sinner is to receive the One Holy God, whom the Seraphim adore with trembling. Thou seest, not only the stains and scars of past sins, but the mutilations, the deep cavities, the chronic disorders which they have left in my soul. Thou seest the innumerable living sins, though they be not mortal, living in their power and presence, their guilt, and their penalties, which clothe me. Thou seest all my bad habits, all my mean principles, all wayward lawless thoughts, my multitude of infirmities and miseries, yet Thou comest. Thou seest most perfectly how little I really feel what I am now saying, yet Thou comest. O my God, left to myself should I not perish under the awful splendor and the consuming fire of Thy Majesty. Enable me to bear Thee, lest I have to say with Peter, "Depart from me, for I am a sinful man, O Lord!" (Luke 5:8).

3. My God, enable me to bear Thee, for Thou alone canst. Cleanse my heart and mind from all that is past. Wipe out clean all my recollections of evil. Rid me from all languor, sickliness, irritability, feebleness of soul. Give me a true perception of things unseen, and make me truly, practically, and in the details of life, prefer Thee to anything on earth, and the future world to the present. Give me courage, a true instinct determining between right and wrong, humility in all things, and a tender longing love of Thee.

The Food of the Soul

"For Thee my soul hath thirsted." (PSALM 63:1)

1. In Thee, O Lord, all things live, and Thou dost give them their food. *Oculi omnium in Te sperant*—"the eyes of all hope in Thee" (Psalm 145:15). To the beasts of the field Thou givest meat and drink. They live on day by day, because Thou dost give them day by day to live. And, if Thou givest not, they feel their misery at once. Nature witnesses to this great truth, for they are visited at once with great agony, and they cry out and wildly wander about, seeking what they need. But, as to us Thy children, Thou feedest us with another food. Thou knowest, O my God, who madest us, that nothing can satisfy us but Thyself, and therefore Thou hast caused Thy own self to be meat and drink to us. O most adorable mystery! O most stupendous of mercies! Thou most Glorious, and Beautiful, and Strong, and Sweet, Thou didst know well that nothing else would support our immortal natures, our frail hearts, but Thyself; and so Thou didst take a human flesh and blood, that they, as being the flesh and blood of God, might be our life.

2. O what an awful thought! Thou dealest otherwise with others, but, as to me, the flesh and blood of God is my sole life. I shall perish without it; yet shall I not perish with it and by it? How can I raise myself to such an act as to feed upon God? O my God, I am in a strait—shall I go forward, or shall I go back? I will go forward: I will go to meet Thee. I will open my mouth, and receive Thy gift. I do so with great awe and fear, but what else can I do? to whom should I go but to Thee? Who can save me but Thou? Who can cleanse me but Thou? Who can make me overcome myself but Thou? Who can raise my body from the grave but Thou? Therefore, I come to Thee in all these my necessities, in fear, but in faith.

3. My God, Thou art my life; if I leave Thee, I cannot but thirst. Lost spirits thirst in hell, because they have not God. They thirst, though they fain would have it otherwise, from the necessity of their original nature. But I, my God, wish to thirst for Thee with a better thirst. I wish to be clad in that new nature, which so longs for Thee from loving Thee, as to overcome in me the fear of coming to Thee. I come to Thee, O Lord, not only because I am unhappy without Thee, not only because I feel I need Thee, but because Thy grace draws me on to seek Thee for Thy own sake, because Thou art so glorious and beautiful. I come in great fear, but in greater love. O may I never lose, as years pass away, and the heart shuts up, and all things are a burden, let me never lose this youthful, eager, elastic love of Thee. Make Thy grace supply the failure of nature. Do the more for me, the less I can do for myself. The more I refuse to open my heart to Thee, so much the fuller and stronger be Thy supernatural visitings, and the more urgent and efficacious Thy presence in me.

XVI
The Sacred Heart

1. O Sacred Heart of Jesus, I adore Thee in the oneness of the Personality of the Second Person of the Holy Trinity. Whatever belongs to the Person of Jesus, belongs therefore to God, and is to be worshipped with that one and the same worship which we pay to Jesus. He did not take on Him His human nature, as something distinct and separate from Himself, but as simply, absolutely, eternally His, so as to be included by us in the very thought of Him. I worship Thee, O Heart of Jesus, as being Jesus Himself, as being that Eternal Word in human nature which He took wholly and lives in wholly, and therefore in Thee. Thou art the Heart of the Most High made man. In worshipping Thee, I worship my Incarnate God, Emmanuel. I worship Thee, as bearing a part in that Passion which is my life, for Thou didst burst and break, through agony, in the garden of Gethsemani, and Thy precious contents trickled out, through the veins and pores of the skin, upon the earth. And again, Thou hadst been drained all but dry upon the Cross; and then, after death, Thou wast pierced by the lance, and gavest out the small remains of that inestimable treasure, which is our redemption.

2. My God, my Savior, I adore Thy Sacred Heart, for that heart is the seat and source of all Thy tenderest human affections for us sinners. It is the instrument and organ of Thy love. It did beat for us. It yearned over us. It ached for us, and for our salvation. It was on fire through zeal, that the glory of God might be manifested in and by us. It is the channel through which has come to us all Thy overflowing human affection, all Thy Divine Charity towards us. All Thy incomprehensible compassion for us, as God and Man, as our Creator and our Redeemer and Judge, has come to us, and

comes, in one inseparably mingled stream, through that Sacred Heart. O most Sacred symbol and Sacrament of Love, divine and human, in its fullness, Thou didst save me by Thy divine strength, and Thy human affection, and then at length by that wonder-working blood, wherewith Thou didst overflow.

3. O most Sacred, most loving Heart of Jesus, Thou art concealed in the Holy Eucharist, and Thou beatest for us still. Now as then Thou savest, *Desiderio desideravi*—"With desire I have desired." I worship Thee then with all my best love and awe, with my fervent affection, with my most subdued, most resolved will. O my God, when Thou dost condescend to suffer me to receive Thee, to eat and drink Thee, and Thou for a while takest up Thy abode within me, O make my heart beat with Thy Heart. Purify it of all that is earthly, all that is proud and sensual, all that is hard and cruel, of all perversity, of all disorder, of all deadness. So, fill it with Thee, that neither the events of the day nor the circumstances of the time may have power to ruffle it, but that in Thy love and Thy fear it may have peace.

XVII
The Infinite Perfection of God

Ex ipso, et per ipsum, et in ipso sunt omnia.
"For of him, and by him, and in him, are all things: to him be glory forever." (ROMANS 11:36)

1. *Ex ipso.* I adore Thee, O my God, as the origin and source of all that is in the world. Once nothing was in being but Thou. It was so for a whole eternity. Thou alone hast had no beginning. Thou hast ever been in being without beginning. Thou hast necessarily been

a whole eternity by Thyself, having in Thee all perfections stored up in Thyself, by Thyself; a world of worlds; an infinite abyss of all that is great and wonderful, beautiful and holy; a treasury of infinite attributes, all in one; infinitely one while thus infinitely various. My God, the thought simply exceeds a created nature, much more mine. I cannot attain to it; I can but use the words, and say "I believe," without comprehending. But this I can do. I can adore Thee, O my great and good God, as the one source of all perfection, and that I do, and with Thy grace will do always.

2. *Per ipsum.* And when other beings began to be, they lived through Thee. They did not begin of themselves. They did not come into existence except by Thy determinate will, by Thy eternal counsel, by Thy sole operation. They are wholly from Thee. From eternity, in the deep ocean of Thy blessedness, Thou didst predestinate everything which in its hour took place. Not a substance, ever so insignificant, but is Thy design and Thy work. Much more, not a soul comes into being, but by Thy direct appointment and act. Thou seest, Thou hast seen from all eternity, every individual of Thy creatures. Thou hast seen me, O my God, from all eternity. Thou seest distinctly, and ever hast seen, whether I am to be saved or to be lost. Thou seest my history through all ages in heaven or in hell. O awful thought! My God, enable me to bear it, lest the thought of Thee confound me utterly; and lead me forward to salvation.

3. *In ipso.* And I believe and know, moreover, that all things live in Thee. Whatever there is of being, of life, of excellence, of enjoyment, of happiness, in the whole creation, is, in its substance, simply and absolutely Thine. It is by dipping into the ocean of Thy infinite perfections that all beings have whatever they have of good. All the beautifulness and majesty of the visible world is a shadow or a glimpse of Thee, or the manifestation or operation in a created medium of one or other of Thy attributes. All that is wonderful

in the way of talent or genius is but an unworthy reflection of the faintest gleam of the Eternal Mind. Whatever we do well, is not only by Thy help, but is after all scarcely an imitation of that sanctity which is in fullness in Thee. O my God, shall I one day see Thee? what sight can compare to that great sight! Shall I see the source of that grace which enlightens me, strengthens me, and consoles me? As I came from Thee, as I am made through Thee, as I live in Thee, so, O my God, may I at last return to Thee, and be with Thee forever and ever.

XVIII
THE INFINITE KNOWLEDGE OF GOD

"All things are naked and open to his eyes; neither is there any creature invisible in his sight." (HEBREWS 4:13)

1. My God, I adore Thee, as beholding all things. Thou knowest in a way altogether different and higher than any knowledge which can belong to creatures. We know by means of sight and thought; there are few things we know in any other way; but how unlike this knowledge, not only in extent, but in its nature and its characteristics, is Thy knowledge! The Angels know many things, but their knowledge compared to Thine is mere ignorance. The human soul, which Thou didst take into Thyself when Thou didst become man, was filled from the first with all the knowledge possible to human nature: but even that was nothing but a drop compared to the abyss of that knowledge, and its keen luminousness, which is Thine as God.

2. My God, could it be otherwise? for from the first and from everlasting Thou wast by Thyself; and Thy blessedness consisted in knowing and contemplating Thyself, the Father in the Son and

Spirit, and the Son and Spirit severally in each other and in the Father, thus infinitely comprehending the infinite. If Thou didst know Thy infinite self thus perfectly, Thou didst know that which was greater and more than anything else could be. All that the whole universe contains, put together, is after all but finite. It is finite, though it be illimitable! it is finite, though it be so multiform; it is finite, though it be so marvelously skillful, beautiful, and magnificent; but Thou art the infinite God, and, knowing Thyself, much more dost Thou know the whole universe, however vast, however intricate and various, and all that is in it.

3.   My great God, Thou knowest all that is in the universe, because Thou Thyself didst make it. It is the very work of Thy hands. Thou art Omniscient, because Thou art omni-creative. Thou knowest each part, however minute, as perfectly as Thou knowest the whole. Thou knowest mind as perfectly as Thou knowest matter. Thou knowest the thoughts and purposes of every soul as perfectly as if there were no other soul in the whole of Thy creation. Thou knowest me through and through; all my present, past, and future are before Thee as one whole. Thou seest all those delicate and evanescent motions of my thought which altogether escape myself. Thou canst trace every act, whether deed or thought, to its origin, and canst follow it into its whole growth, to its origin, and canst follow it into its whole growth and consequences. Thou knowest how it will be with me at the end; Thou hast before Thee that hour when I shall come to Thee to be judged. How awful is the prospect of finding myself in the presence of my Judge! Yet, O Lord, I would not that Thou shouldst not know me. It is my greatest stay to know that Thou readest my heart. O give me more of that open-hearted sincerity which I have desired. Keep me ever from being afraid of Thy eye, from the inward consciousness that I am not honestly trying to please Thee. Teach me to love Thee more, and then I shall be at peace, without any fear of Thee at all.

XIX
The Providence of God

1. I adore Thee, my God, as having laid down the ends and the means of all things which Thou hast created. Thou hast created everything for some end of its own, and Thou dost direct it to that end. The end, which Thou didst in the beginning appoint for man, is Thy worship and service, and his own happiness in paying it; a blessed eternity of soul and body with Thee forever. Thou hast provided for this, and that in the case of every man. As Thy hand and eye are upon the brute creation, so are they upon us. Thou sustainest everything in life and action for its own end. Not a reptile, not an insect, but Thou seest and makest to live, while its time lasts. Not a sinner, not an idolater, not a blasphemer, not an atheist lives, but by Thee, and in order that he may repent. Thou art careful and tender to each of the beings that Thou hast created, as if it were the only one in the whole world. For Thou canst see every one of them at once, and Thou lovest everyone in this mortal life, and pursuest everyone by itself, with all the fullness of Thy attributes, as if Thou wast waiting on it and ministering to it for its own sake. My God, I love to contemplate Thee, I love to adore Thee, thus the wonderful worker of all things every day in every place.

2. All Thy acts of providence are acts of love. If Thou sendest evil upon us, it is in love. All the evils of the physical world are intended for the good of Thy creatures, or are the unavoidable attendants on that good. And Thou turnest that evil into good. Thou visitest men with evil to bring them to repentance, to increase their virtue, to gain for them greater good hereafter. Nothing is done in vain, but has its gracious end. Thou dost punish, yet in wrath Thou dost remember mercy. Even Thy justice when it overtakes the impenitent sinner, who had exhausted Thy loving providences towards him,

is mercy to others, as saving them from his contamination, or granting them a warning. I acknowledge with a full and firm faith, O Lord, the wisdom and goodness of Thy Providence, even in Thy inscrutable judgments and Thy incomprehensible decrees.

3. O my God, my whole life has been a course of mercies and blessings shewn to one who has been most unworthy of them. I require no faith, for I have had long experience, as to Thy providence towards me. Year after year Thou hast carried me on—removed dangers from my path—recovered me, recruited me, refreshed me, borne with me, directed me, sustained me. O forsake me not when my strength faileth me. And Thou never wilt forsake me. I may securely repose upon Thee. Sinner as I am, nevertheless, while I am true to Thee, Thou wilt still and to the end, be superabundantly true to me. I may rest upon Thy arm; I may go to sleep in Thy bosom. Only give me, and increase in me, that true loyalty to Thee, which is the bond of the covenant between Thee and me, and the pledge in my own heart and conscience that Thou, the Supreme God, wilt not forsake me, the most miserable of Thy children.

XX
GOD IS ALL IN ALL

"One God and Father of all, who is above all, and through all, and in us all." (Ephesians 4:6)

1. God alone is in heaven; God is all in all. Eternal Lord, I acknowledge this truth, and I adore Thee in this sovereign and most glorious mystery. There is One God, and He fills heaven; and all blessed creatures, though they ever remain in their individuality, are, as the very means of their blessedness, absorbed, and (as it were)

drowned in the fullness of Him who is *super omnes, et per omnia, et in omnibus.* If ever, through Thy grace, I attain to see Thee in heaven, I shall see nothing else but Thee, because I shall see all whom I see in Thee, and seeing them I shall see Thee. As I cannot see things here below without light, and to see them is to see the rays which come from them, so in that Eternal City *claritas Dei illuminavit eam, et lucerna ejus est Agnus*—the glory of God hath enlightened it, and the Lamb is the lamp thereof. My God, I adore Thee now (at least I will do so to the best of my powers) as the One Sole True Life and Light of the soul, as I shall know and see Thee to be hereafter, if by Thy grace I attain to heaven.

2. Eternal, Incomprehensible God, I believe, and confess, and adore Thee, as being infinitely more wonderful, resourceful, and immense, than this universe which I see. I look into the depths of space, in which the stars are scattered about, and I understand that I should be millions upon millions of years in creeping along from one end of it to the other, if a bridge were thrown across it. I consider the overpowering variety, richness, intricacy of Thy work; the elements, principles, laws, results which go to make it up. I try to recount the multitudes of kinds of knowledge, of sciences, and of arts of which it can be made the subject. And, I know, I should be ages upon ages in learning everything that is to be learned about this world, supposing me to have the power of learning it at all. And new sciences would come to light, at present unsuspected, as fast as I had mastered the old, and the conclusions of today would be nothing more than starting points of tomorrow. And I see moreover, and the more I examined it, the more I should understand, the marvelous beauty of these works of Thy hands. And so, I might begin again, after this material universe, and find a new world of knowledge, higher and more wonderful, in Thy intellectual creations, Thy angels and other spirits, and men. But

all, all that is in these worlds, high and low, are but an atom compared with the grandeur, the height and depth, the glory, on which Thy saints are gazing in their contemplation of Thee. It is the occupation of eternity, ever new, inexhaustible, ineffably ecstatic, the stay and the blessedness of existence, thus to drink in and be dissolved in Thee.

3. My God, it was Thy supreme blessedness in the eternity past, as it is Thy blessedness in all eternities, to know Thyself, as Thou alone canst know Thee. It was by seeing Thyself in Thy Co-equal Son and Thy Co-eternal Spirit, and in Their seeing Thee, that Father, Son, and Holy Ghost, Three Persons, One God, was infinitely blessed. O my God, what am I that Thou shouldst make my blessedness to consist in that which is Thy own! That Thou shouldst grant me to have not only the sight of Thee, but to share in Thy very own joy! O prepare me for it, teach me to thirst for it.

XXI
GOD THE INCOMMUNICABLE PERFECTION

1. Almighty God, Thou art the One Infinite Fullness. From eternity, Thou art the One and only absolute and most all-sufficient seat and proper abode of all conceivable best attributes, and of all, which are many more, which cannot be conceived. I hold this as a matter of reason, though my imagination starts from it. I hold it firmly and absolutely, though it is the most difficult of all mysteries. I hold it from the actual experience of Thy blessings and mercies towards me, the evidences of Thy awful Being and attributes, brought home continually to my reason, beyond the power of doubting or disputing. I hold it from that long and intimate familiarity with it, so that it is part of my rational nature to hold it; because I am

so constituted and made up upon the idea of it, as a keystone, that not to hold it would be to break my mind to pieces. I hold it from that intimate perception of it in my conscience, as a fact present to me, that I feel it as easy to deny my own personality as the personality of God, and have lost my grounds for believing that I exist myself, if I deny existence to Him. I hold it because I could not bear to be without Thee, O my Lord and Life, because I look for blessings beyond thought by being with Thee. I hold it from the terror of being left in this wild world without stay or protection. I hold it from humble love to Thee, from delight in Thy glory and exaltation, from my desire that Thou shouldst be great and the only great one. I hold it for Thy sake, and because I love to think of Thee as so glorious, perfect, and beautiful. There is one God, and none other but He.

2. Since, O Eternal God, Thou art so incommunicably great, so one, so perfect in that oneness, surely one would say, Thou ever must be most distant from Thy creatures, didst Thou create any—separated from them by Thy eternal ancientness on their beginning to be, and separated by Thy transcendency of excellence and Thy absolute contrariety to them. What couldst Thou give them out of Thyself, which would suit their nature, so different from Thine? What good of Thine could be their good, or do them good, except in some poor external way? If Thou couldst be the happiness of man, then might man in turn, or some gift from him, be the happiness of the bird of prey or the wild beast, the cattle of his pasture, or the myriads of minute creatures which we can scarcely see. Man is not so far above them, as Thou above him. For what is every creature in Thy sight, O Lord, but a vanity and a breath, a smoke which stays not, but flits by and passes away, a poor thing which only vanishes so much the sooner, because Thou lookest on it, and it is set in the illumination of Thy countenance? Is not this, O Lord,

the perplexity of reason? From the Perfect comes the Perfect; yet Thou canst not make a second God, from the nature of the case; and therefore, either canst not create at all, or of necessity must create what is infinitely unlike, and therefore, in a sense, unworthy of the Creator.

3. What communion then can there be between Thee and me? O my God! what am I but a parcel of dead bones, a feeble, tottering, miserable being, compared with Thee. I am Thy work, and Thou didst create me pure from sin, but how canst Thou look upon me in my best estate of nature, with complacency? how canst Thou see in me any image of Thyself, the Creator? How is this, my Lord? Thou didst pronounce Thy work very good, and didst make man in Thy image. Yet there is an infinite gulf between Thee and me, O my God.

XXII
GOD COMMUNICATED TO US

1. Thou hast, O Lord, an incommunicable perfection, but still that Omnipotence by which Thou didst create, is sufficient also to the work of communicating Thyself to the spirits which Thou hast created. Thy Almighty Life is not for our destruction, but for our living. Thou remainest ever one and the same in Thyself, but there goes from Thee continually a power and virtue, which by its contact is our strength and good. I do not know how this can be; my reason does not satisfy me here; but in nature I see intimations, and by faith I have full assurance of the truth of this mystery. By Thee we cross the gulf that lies between Thee and us. The Living God is lifegiving. Thou art the Fount and Center, as well as the Seat, of all good. The traces of Thy glory, as the many-colored rays

of the sun, are scattered over the whole face of nature, without diminution of Thy perfections, or violation of Thy transcendent and unapproachable Essence. How it can be, I know not; but so it is. And thus, remaining one and sole and infinitely removed from all things, still Thou art the fullness of all things, in Thee they consist, of Thee they partake, and into Thee, retaining their own individuality, they are absorbed. And thus, while we droop and decay in our own nature, we live by Thy breath; and Thy grace enables us to endure Thy presence.

2. Make me then like Thyself, O my God, since, in spite of myself, such Thou canst make me, such I can be made. Look on me, O my Creator, pity the work of Thy hands, *ne peream in infirmitate mea*—"that I perish not in my infirmity." Take me out of my natural imbecility, since that is possible for me, which is so necessary. Thou hast shewn it to be possible in the face of the whole world by the most overwhelming proof, by taking our created nature on Thyself, and exalting it in Thee. Give me in my own self the benefit of this wondrous truth, now it has been so publicly ascertained and guaranteed. Let me have in my own person, what in Jesus Thou hast given to my nature. Let me be partaker of that Divine Nature in all the riches of Its attributes, which in fullness of substance and in personal presence became the Son of Mary. Give me that life, suitable to my own need, which is stored up for us all in Him who is the Life of men. Teach me and enable me to live the life of Saints and Angels. Take me out of the languor, the irritability, the sensitiveness, the incapability, the anarchy, in which my soul lies, and fill it with Thy fullness. Breathe on me, that the dead bones may live. Breathe on me with that Breath which infuses energy and kindles fervor. In asking for fervor, I ask for all that I can need, and all that Thou canst give; for it is the crown of all gifts and all virtues. It cannot really and fully be, except where all are

at present. It is the beauty and the glory, as it is also the continual safeguard and purifier of them all. In asking for fervor, I am asking for effectual strength, consistency, and perseverance; I am asking for deadness to every human motive, and simplicity of intention to please Thee: I am asking for faith, hope, and charity in their most heavenly exercise. In asking for fervor I am asking to be rid of the fear of man, and the desire of his praise; I am asking for the gift of prayer, because it will be so sweet; I am asking for that loyal perception of duty, which follows on yearning affection; I am asking for sanctity, peace, and joy all at once. In asking for fervor, I am asking for the brightness of the Cherubim and the fire of the Seraphim, and the whiteness of all Saints. In asking for fervor, I am asking for that which, while it implies all gifts, is that in which I signally fail. Nothing would be a trouble to me, nothing a difficulty, had I but fervor of soul.

3. Lord, in asking for fervor, I am asking for Thyself, for nothing short of Thee, O my God, who hast given Thyself wholly to us. Enter my heart substantially and personally, and fill it with fervor by filling it with Thee. Thou alone canst fill the soul of man, and Thou hast promised to do so. Thou art the living Flame, and ever burnest with love of man: enter into me and set me on fire after Thy pattern and likeness.

XXIII
GOD THE SOLE STAY FOR ETERNITY

1. My God, I believe and know and adore Thee as infinite in the multiplicity and depth of Thy attributes. I adore Thee as containing in Thee an abundance of all that can delight and satisfy the soul. I know, on the contrary, and from sad experience I am too sure, that

whatever is created, whatever is earthly, pleases but for the time, and then palls and is a weariness. I believe that there is nothing at all here below, which I should not at length get sick of. I believe, that, though I had all the means of happiness which this life could give, yet in time I should tire of living, feeling everything trite and dull and unprofitable. I believe, that, were it my lot to live the long antediluvian life, and to live it without Thee, I should be utterly, inconceivably, wretched at the end of it. I think I should be tempted to destroy myself for very weariness and disgust. I think I should at last lose my reason and go mad, if my life here was prolonged long enough. I should feel it like solitary confinement, for I should find myself shut up in myself without companion, if I could not converse with Thee, my God. Thou only, O my Infinite Lord, art ever new, though Thou art the ancient of days—the last as well as the first.

2. Thou, O my God, art ever new, though Thou art the most ancient—Thou alone art the food for eternity. I am to live forever, not for a time—and I have no power over my being; I cannot destroy myself, even though I were so wicked as to wish to do so. I must live on, with intellect and consciousness forever, in spite of myself. Without Thee eternity would be another name for eternal misery. In Thee alone have I that which can stay me up for ever: Thou alone art the food of my soul. Thou alone art inexhaustible, and ever offerest to me something new to know, something new to love. At the end of millions of years, I shall know Thee so little, that I shall seem to myself only beginning. At the end of millions of years, I shall find in Thee the same, or rather, greater sweetness than at first, and shall seem then only to be beginning to enjoy Thee: and so on for eternity I shall ever be a little child beginning to be taught the rudiments of Thy infinite Divine nature. For Thou art Thyself the seat and center of all good, and the only substance

in this universe of shadows, and the heaven in which blessed spirits live and rejoice.

3. My God, I take Thee for my portion. From mere prudence I turn from the world to Thee; I give up the world for Thee. I renounce that which promises for Him who performs. To whom else should I go? I desire to find and feed on Thee here; I desire to feed on Thee, Jesu, my Lord, who art risen, who hast gone up on high, who yet remainest with Thy people on earth. I look up to Thee; I look for the Living Bread which is in heaven, which comes down from heaven. Give me ever of this Bread. Destroy this life, which will soon perish—even though Thou dost not destroy it, and fill me with that supernatural life, which will never die.

CONCLUSION
WRITTEN IN PROSPECT OF DEATH

March 13th, 1864, Passion Sunday, 7 o'clock A.M.

I write in the direct view of death as in prospect. No one in the house, I suppose, suspects anything of the kind. Nor anyone anywhere, unless it be the medical men.

I write at once, because, on my own feelings of mind and body, it is as if nothing at all were the matter with me, just now; but because I do not know how long this perfect possession of my sensible and available health and strength may last.

I die in the faith of the One Holy Catholic Apostolic Church. I trust I shall die prepared and protected by her Sacraments, which our Lord Jesus Christ has committed to her, and in that communion of Saints which He inaugurated when He ascended on high, and which will have no end. I hope to die in that Church which our Lord founded on Peter, and which will continue till His second coming.

I commit my soul and body to the Most Holy Trinity, and to the merits and grace of our Lord Jesus, God Incarnate, to the intercession and compassion of our dear Mother Mary; to St. Joseph; and St. Philip Neri, my father, the father of an unworthy son; to St. John the Evangelist; St. John the Baptist; St. Henry; St. Athanasius, and St. Gregory Nazianzen; to St. Chrysostom, and St. Ambrose.

Also to St. Peter, St. Gregory I, and St. Leo. Also to the great Apostle St. Paul.

Also to my tender Guardian Angel, and to all Angels, and to all Saints.

And I pray to God to bring us all together again in heaven, under the feet of the Saints. And, after the pattern of Him, who seeks so diligently for those who are astray, I would ask Him especially to have mercy on those who are external to the True Fold, and to bring them into it before they die.

J. H. N.